SCHOLASTIC AMERICAN CITIZENSHIP

Revised Edition

Advisory Editors

James MacGregor Burns
Professor of Political Science
Williams College

Hadley P. Arkes
Associate Professor of Political Science
Amherst College

Philippa Strum
Professor of Political Science
Brooklyn College of the City University
of New York

Educational Consultants

Jean Tilford Claugus
Past President of the National
Council for the Social Studies

Ann-Marie Brush
Coordinator of Social Studies Instruction
Brevard County, Florida

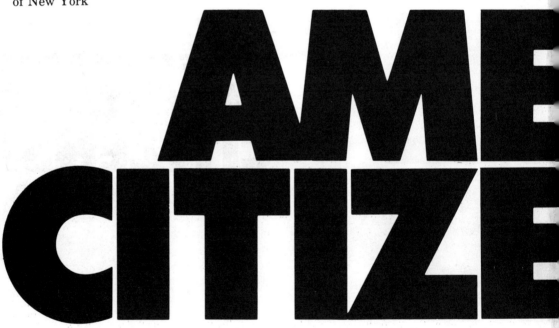

by **Steven Jantzen,
Carolyn Jackson,
Norman Lunger,
Diana Reische, and
Phillip Parker**

SCHOLASTIC
[AME]RICAN
[CITIZE]NSHIP

Revised Edition

Scholastic Book Services

New York   Toronto   London   Sydney   Auckland   Tokyo

Teaching Consultants:

Terry Erickson
Sylvan Intermediate School
Citrus Heights, California

Dean A. Woelfle
East Peoria High School
East Peoria, Illinois

Mary Ann Brady
Bass Junior High School
Nashville, Tennessee

Staff for the
SCHOLASTIC AMERICAN
CITIZENSHIP PROGRAM:

Project Editors: Charles L. Wrye,
Stephen M. Lewin
Editorial Director: William F. Goodykoontz
Editorial Assistants: Jonathan Landman,
Phillip Parker, Carolyn Jackson,
Elvira Pedernales, William Johnson,
Perry Morse
Readability Consultant: Lawrence B. Charry

Production Editor: Nancy J. Smith

Art Editor and Designer: David Rollert
Art Director: Dale Moyer
Maps: Hal Aber
Collages: Gary Friedman
Illustrations: Gerry Gersten, Mario Jamora
Unit Dividers, Part Two: Hans Georg Rauch

For reprint permission, grateful acknowledgment is
made to:

American Enterprise Institute, 1150 17th St. N.W.,
Washington, DC 20036, for the chart "Summary of
Political Systems & Electoral Laws" from
ELECTORAL REFORM AND VOTER
PARTICIPATION by Phillips and Blackman.

Collins-World Publishers, Inc., for an excerpt from
TRADITION AND CHANGE IN AFRICAN
TRIBAL LIFE by Colin M. Turnbull.

Crown Publishers, Inc., for excerpts from APRIL
MORNING by Howard Fast, ©1961 by Howard Fast,
and THE NEW POLITICS by James Perry, ©1968
by James Perry.

Joan Daves for the excerpts from "I Have a Dream"
by Martin Luther King, Jr., copyright © 1963 by
Martin Luther King, Jr.

Doubleday & Company, Inc., for the adapted excerpt
from THEY ALSO RAN by Irving Stone, copyright
1943 by Irving Stone; and for the excerpts from
THE CAINE MUTINY by Herman Wouk, copyright
©1954 by Herman Wouk, and TO BE A
POLITICIAN by Stimson Bullitt, copyright ©1959
by Stimson Bullitt.

Friends of the Earth for the excerpt by Kenneth P.
Cantor from THE ENVIRONMENTAL
HANDBOOK, edited by Garrett DeBell, ©Garrett
DeBell, published by Ballantine Books.

Gordian Press, Inc., for the adapted excerpt from
CONGRESS ON TRIAL by James MacGregor
Burns.

Grossman Publishers, a division of The Viking
Press, Inc., for an excerpt from WHO RUNS
CONGRESS? by Mark J. Green, James M. Fallows,
and David R. Zwick, copyright ©1972 by Ralph
Nader.

CONTENTS

PART ONE: FOUNDATIONS OF OUR GOVERNMENT, 10

PART TWO: THE PRESIDENCY, CONGRESS, AND THE SUPREME COURT, 192

PART THREE: STATE AND LOCAL GOVERNMENT, 404

PART FOUR: POLITICS AND PEOPLE, 602

Maps and Charts

PART ONE: FOUNDATIONS OF OUR GOVERNMENT

UNIT I: GOVERNMENT BY THE PEOPLE

1: WHY DO WE NEED GOVERNMENT?

Suppose you are watching a great, old movie about *mutiny** at sea—*The Caine Mutiny*. On the screen, you see the frightened face of Humphrey Bogart, the movie's starring actor. Bogart plays the part of a Navy captain, Captain Queeg. The ship under his command is the *U.S.S. Caine*.

The Caine Mutiny has been a popular novel and a successful movie, but it is more than a good story. It's also

a good study of government. It helps to explain why human groups throughout the world need some form of government. A ship of 200 men needs to be governed. So does a school of 1,000 students. So does a nation of 230 million people. Why?

To find out why, read the following dramatic moment in the story of the *Caine*. In the scene, the ship is pitching helplessly in a stormy sea. Strong winds and giant waves threaten the ship with destruction. A sailor named Stilwell is at the helm (the wheel controlling the rudder of the ship for

---

*See the Glossary for the definition. (All starred, *italicized* words are in the Glossary.)

steering). With him are Captain Queeg and Steve Maryk. Maryk is the ship's *executive** officer. He's second-in-command under Queeg. The hero of the story, Willie Keith, is also present in the ship's wheelhouse.

The scene as presented here is adapted from the book *The Caine Mutiny:*

"[Compass] heading 245, sir." Stilwell's voice was sobbing. "She ain't answering engines at all, sir!"

The *Caine* rolled almost completely over on its port [left] side. Everybody in the wheelhouse except Stilwell went sliding across the streaming deck and piled up against the windows. The sea was under their noses, dashing up against the glass.

"Mr. Maryk, the light on this gyro [compass] just went out!" screamed Stilwell, clinging desperately to the wheel.

"Reverse your rudder, Stilwell! Hard right! Hard right!" cried the exec harshly.

"Hard right, sir!"

Maryk crawled across the deck, threw himself on the engine-room telegraph,[1] wrested the handles from Queeg's weak grip, and reversed the settings. "Excuse me, Captain — ?" A horrible coughing rumble came from the stacks. "What's your head?" barked Maryk.

"Two seven five, sir!"

"Hold her at hard right!"

"Aye, aye, sir!"

The old minesweeper rolled up a little from the surface of the water. Until now, the wind had been turning the ship from south to west. Queeg had been trying to fight back to south. Maryk was doing just the opposite now. He was trying to swing the ship's head completely northward, into the wind and sea.

---

[1] A tall upright device with handles by which signals (settings) are sent from the wheelhouse to the engine room. These settings help determine speed and direction.

Queeg, Maryk, and Stilwell

Willie had lost all awareness of the captain's presence. Maryk had filled his mind as father, leader, and savior. He looked now at Queeg, a little pale man who stood with arms and legs entwined around the telegraph stand. Willie had the feeling that Queeg was a stranger.

The captain, blinking and shaking his head as though he had just awakened, said, "Come left to 180."

"Sir, we can't ride stern to wind and save this ship," said the exec.

"Left to 180, helmsman."

"Hold it, Stilwell," said Maryk.

"Mr. Maryk, fleet course is 180." The captain's voice was faint, almost whispering. He was looking glassily ahead. "We're not in trouble," said Queeg. "Come left to 180."

"Steady as you go!" said Maryk, at the same instant. The helmsman looked around from one officer to the other, his eyes popping in panic. "Do as I say," shouted the executive officer. He strode to the captain's side and saluted. "Captain, I'm sorry, sir, you're a sick man. I am temporarily relieving you of this ship under Article 184 of *Navy Regulations*."

"I don't know what you're talking about," said Queeg. "Left to 180, helmsman."

"What should I do?" cried Stilwell.

Government and group survival.
How does that argument in the middle of a storm help us to understand the need for government? Notice three things about the scene. First, the survival of the ship and all the men aboard depends on how well the

ship is steered. Second, there is confusion at the helm. Stilwell is uncertain whether to head north or south. Third, confusion and divided leadership at the helm are as dangerous as the storm itself. The ship *must* be steered in *some* direction; otherwise it will surely be lost.

People best realize what government is when they begin to lose it. For one moment on the *Caine,* there was no government at all for the ship. It was the moment when the helmsman, Stilwell, was unsure whom he should obey. Before this, everyone on the ship understood that the captain was in charge.

Among other things, government is a system for giving leadership and direction to a group. When that system breaks down, there is disorder and confusion. And that is what happened on the *Caine* when Captain Queeg faltered and his authority was challenged by Maryk, the executive officer.

But *democratic** government is much more than a system to provide leadership. It is a way for individuals with many differences to join together for the good of all. It is a means by which people make and carry out laws to keep order and protect rights. Perhaps the Declaration of Independence says it best:

"We hold these truths to be self-evident, that all men . . . are endowed by their Creator with certain *unalienable** rights, that among these are

life, liberty, and the pursuit of happiness. That to secure these rights governments are instituted. . . ."

On the *Caine,* because of the failure of leadership during the storm, all three basic rights were in danger.

What would the U.S. be like without government? Like most groups, the United States has a system of government to take care of its different needs. Imagine what our country might be like without a government. Here are nine possibilities of what *might* happen if there were no government in the United States. Which of these do you think would probably happen? Which do you think would probably *not* happen? Why?

1. There would be no way to settle arguments fairly and peacefully. Thefts and murders would be much more common than they are today.

2. Big businesses — such as TV, movies, airlines, car manufacturing, and the like — could not exist.

3. People would be free to do what they wanted. Life would be simpler and more fun for everyone.

4. Almost everyone would be armed. People would be so busy defending themselves and their *property** that there would be little time for growing food or building houses or educating children.

5. The country would be invaded by foreign armies. We would be easily conquered by any foreign government that wished to rule us.

6. Most people would be terribly poor. Many would starve to death. Many old, blind, and sick people would be without help.

7. There would be only two kinds of Americans. One group would have all the power and the money. The other much larger group would have almost nothing. There would be no freedom for most Americans.

8. People would still be basically good and would get along better without *politicians** and police.

9. The situation wouldn't last long. Without government, conditions would be so terrible that people would get together all over the country and begin to set up governments to make life safer and better for all.

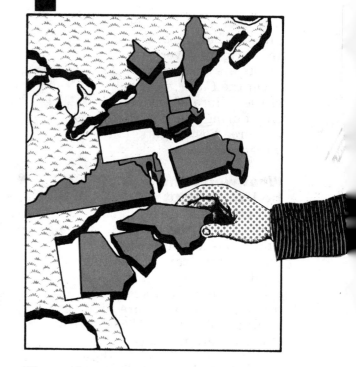

Six main purposes of the U.S. government. There was a time, as you know, when the United States did not exist. But in 1776 the 13 North American *colonies** of Great Britain declared their independence from that country. They set up a new nation, the United States of America.

And in 1787 the United States government was organized into the kind of system we have today. That system was explained in a written document called the U.S. *Constitution*.* The first sentence of the Constitution is the most famous part of it. It's called the *Preamble*.* The Preamble begins: "We, the people of the United States . . . "; and it ends ". . . establish this Constitution for the United States of America." Thus,

in its first sentence, the Constitution states the most important fact about our government: All of its power comes from the people.

In between "We, the people" and "establish this Constitution," the Preamble lists six main purposes of our government. Each purpose is explained as follows:

1. To "form a more perfect union." The men who wrote the Constitution in 1787 had been living in a weak "union" of 13 states created under the *Articles of Confederation.** You will read more about this in Chapter 5.

These men agreed on the need for a stronger national government — "a more perfect union" of the states. But this phrase suggests more than a stronger political union. It suggests the need for a government which could unite people in the different parts of the country to work together for the good of all. In time it has come to mean too that the government should do what is necessary so that all citizens of the U.S. should feel that they are equal members of the nation.

2. To "establish justice." In all societies, people need to have peaceful and orderly ways to settle disputes. A citizen believes his rights have been violated by the local sheriff. A business in one state claims that a business in another state has violated a *contract** between them. One of the purposes of government is to settle such quarrels in

a just way without violence. But for justice to exist, all citizens must believe that the government will play no favorites.

3. To "insure domestic tranquility." One important purpose of a government is to keep all citizens safe from violence and disorder, so that they may go about their normal business. The states have the primary duty of keeping order, but crime often crosses state lines. People want to be sure that their property and their lives are safe and that their liberties are protected. So they join together to form a government strong enough to achieve these goals.

4. To "provide for the common defense." If the United States had no government, there would be no national armed forces — no Army, Navy, or Air Force. Would the lack of a nationwide system of defense tempt other nations to attack us? Many people think so. Throughout the history of the world, there have been wars between rival tribes and nations. Therefore, one of the goals of government is to make sure that the country is protected against *military** action by possible enemy forces.

5. To "promote the general welfare." To survive — and to justify surviving — a nation needs to do more than protect its citizens from crime and war. People also need ways to help each other during natural disasters such as fires, floods, hurricanes, and tornadoes. They need a system to enable them

6

to share the burdens of bad harvests and famines. In case of sickness or injury, individuals need health care. To hold a good job and to "pursue happiness" on an equal basis, they usually need to learn basic skills — such as reading and writing. Private *agencies** and state and local governments often lack the means to care for these needs adequately. Help from the people as a whole — from the national government — may be needed.

6. To "secure the blessings of liberty." When the men who wrote the Constitution put this phrase in, they probably had in mind the freedom of the new country from the harsh rule of Great Britain. But during the years since then, these words have come to mean liberty for individuals — that all Americans should be free to say what they think, to find fault with government leaders without fear of persecution, and to shape their lives as they see fit.

Has the U.S. government succeeded? The U.S. government has tried to fulfill all six purposes listed in the Preamble of the Constitution. But it has succeeded better with some purposes than others. Which of the six purposes do you think our government has carried out best? Which has it been least successful in carrying out? Give reasons for your answers.

Now, think about the needs of our nation today. Of the following needs, which is most important to you? Which seems least important? On a sheet of paper, list each need in the order of its importance to you:

1. The need for more and better highways, more and better airports, more and better post offices.

2. The need for a court system that is fair to all citizens.

3. The need for stronger police protection against crime, rioting, and disorder.

4. The need for a stronger Army, Navy, and Air Force.

5. The need for better schools and hospitals.

6. The need for equal freedom for all American citizens.

What do you think the U.S. government should do to succeed better at the goal you chose as the most important?

You now know six purposes of government listed in the Preamble of the Constitution. Suppose a government fails to achieve one or more of its purposes. In that case, do people have a right to change the government?

That was the real question aboard the *Caine* when the helmsman cried out: "What should I do?" What would you have done in his place? Would you have followed the captain — or Steve Maryk? Before deciding, you should know more about Captain Queeg and his "government" aboard the *Caine*.

Three other scenes from *The Caine Mutiny* are described here. In each scene, you see a different side of the captain and his ability to govern. All three scenes happened *before* the attempt at mutiny in the storm. The captain's actions were widely talked about by the ship's officers and crew.

First, read the three scenes and answer all of the questions about Captain Queeg's "government."

Then, place yourself in the helmsman's boots and answer his question: "What should I do?"

Scene 1: helmets and life jackets. The *Caine* is heading for San Francisco. The men are talking about what they'll do with their two weeks of "liberty" (free time on shore) when they land.

Then Captain Queeg discovers that most of the crew have ignored a Navy rule about wearing helmets and life jackets. Angrily, he announces over the loudspeakers: "Every man who is not wearing a helmet or a life jacket is docked one day's leave in the United States. Every man who is wearing neither is deprived of three days' leave."

The crew reacts in a panic. They scramble to get their helmets and jackets on. This angers the captain even more. He announces that *everyone* is to be docked three days — guilty and innocent alike.

Questions: How is the Captain failing to live up to one or more purposes of government? Which purposes are being ignored in this scene?

Scene 2: battle for a Pacific island. The *Caine* gets orders to support a naval attack against an island held by the Japanese. When the ships get into firing range of the island, Captain Queeg gets nervous. He ducks for cover and orders Steve Maryk to steer the ship. But as the ship gets closer to enemy guns, the captain shouts out another order:

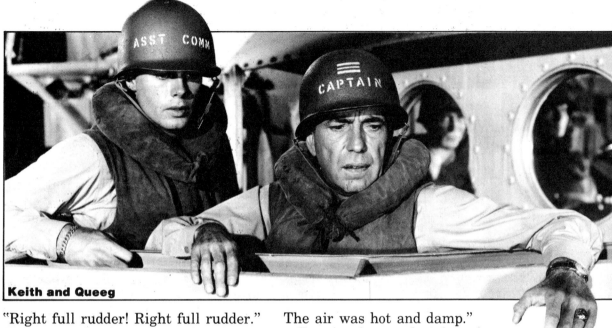

Keith and Queeg

"Right full rudder! Right full rudder." This turns the *Caine* around and heads it out to sea. After that, the Captain is known by a new nickname, "Old Yellowstain."

Question: In this scene, which purpose of government did Captain Queeg fail to live up to?

Scene 3: not a drop to drink.

Captain Queeg discovers that, during the battle, the men had drunk more water than normal. To "teach them a lesson," he forbids anyone to take a shower or a drink of water for 48 hours. This order comes on a summer day, when no wind is blowing and the air is thick with fumes from the ship's smokestacks. The book's author describes the scene like this:

"The stack gas swirled and rolled on the main deck. It stank. It coated tongue and throats with an itchy, foul-tasting film. It stung the eyes.

The air was hot and damp."

For two days and nights, the men suffered terribly from the heat, the gas, and the lack of water.

Questions: In this scene, how did Captain Queeg fail to live up to his responsibilities? Which purpose of government did he ignore?

You're the helmsman. You know Captain Queeg's weaknesses and failings. You know that his weakness may threaten the survival of the ship. But you also know that mutiny threatens the whole system of law and order. It is a crime that can be punished by death — unless there is good cause for it. Knowing this, would you obey Captain Queeg's orders or Steve Maryk's? (To find out what happened in the book and the movie, ask your teacher. The answer is in the Answer Key which is in the Teaching Guide for this book.)

23

"THE LAST WORD"

by Colin M. Turnbull

Justice is one of the purposes of governments in all parts of the world. There are judges, courts, and trials in African villages as well as in American towns and cities. The system of justice in some African tribal villages was studied by a British scholar, Colin M. Turnbull. The reading below is adapted from Turnbull's book Tradition* and Change in African Tribal Life. *From it, you'll discover how an African tribe's ideas of justice compare with the American idea.*

The African judge is often concerned with more than the crime itself. He is interested in the surrounding circumstances. Take a simple case of theft. B steals a chicken from A. So A brings B to court, and B promptly agrees that he did steal the chicken. That would seem to be the end of the case, but far from it. The judge then asks B why he stole the chicken.

The "thief" may be very honest. He may say that he stole the chicken, hoping to force A to bring him to court. This seems even stranger, so

again he is asked why. By now A is beginning to look less sure of himself. B says that his soul was troubled because he thought he had seen A flirting with his wife.

The judge turns to A and asks him if he was indeed flirting with B's wife. If A has a sharp mind he will calmly say yes, and wait to be asked, as usual, why. At that he brings up some old grudge, perhaps not even against B, but against some member of B's family. He says that this made his soul bad and caused him to flirt with B's wife.

More and more people are slowly dragged into the case, which may go on for several days. They all play the same game, bringing out one grudge after another. Now that they are brought out in the open, however, all the harm is gone. Everyone knows that he did not in fact get away with something that he thought had gone unnoticed.

Something else remains to be done. It is important in African society to restore the good feeling that should exist within the family. So, the judge may well give the *verdict** in favor of the man who admitted the theft in the first place! But it is not a simple verdict.

The judge will say A must pay to B (who stole his chicken!) a goat. A looks pretty dismal. But the judge continues, saying that it is bad for a man to eat a goat alone. So B must share the goat with A. Further, B's family caused A's soul to be hurt. So they must get together and brew some beer to be given to A. But it is

24

bad to drink beer alone, so A must share with B!

In the end, A and B have to get together, brew beer, and roast a goat. Then they sit down together and jointly share the feast, a sign of sure friendship! Something much more important has been achieved than if A had gotten his chicken back. Good feeling has been restored.

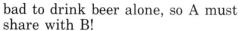

(YOU HAVE THE LAST WORD)

What's your opinion of the African tribe's system of justice? Is it a good way or a poor way to settle conflicts between people? Would a system like this work well in America? For example, suppose Mr. C steals Mrs. D's diamond ring. How do American judges usually deal with such a problem?

"CHECKOUT"

Key terms

government
democratic
unalienable rights
politician
colonies
Constitution

form a more perfect union
establish justice
insure domestic tranquility
provide for the common defense
promote the general welfare
secure the blessings of liberty

Review

1. Complete these statements:
(a) Democratic government is much more than a system to provide leadership. It is a way for individuals with many differences to ———— .
(b) It is a means by which people make ———— .

2. List three basic rights which the Declaration of Independence says are among the "unalienable" rights of all people.

3. According to the Declaration of Independence, "governments are instituted" for what reason?

4. What are the first three words and the last nine words of the Preamble to the U.S. Constitution?

5. List the six main purposes of our government as stated in the Preamble, and for each purpose give one reason that helps to explain its meaning.

Discussion

1. Among the "unalienable rights" specifically named in the Declaration of Independence is the "pursuit of happiness." What does it mean? Your class might brainstorm answers while someone writes them on the chalkboard. (State as many ideas as you can think of as they occur to you.) Afterward, strike out all duplicates and those that are clearly out of bounds. Then evaluate the others, and choose the three or four statements that, in your judgment, best explain what the authors of the Declaration of Independence meant by "pursuit of happiness."

2. Comment on — attack, defend, or amend (until it expresses your view) — this statement: *That we need government does not necessarily mean that the more government we have, the better off we will be. It was the author of the Declaration of Independence who also wrote: "I am not a friend of very energetic government. It is always oppressive."*

3. All governments — even democratic governments — need good leaders. You might choose five students to conduct a panel discussion on the topic: *What makes a good leader?*

The panel should have a chairperson to keep the discussion flowing in an orderly way. Each member should follow a time limit (usually no more than three minutes) for her or his presentation. One panel member might discuss qualities that a good leader should *not* have, perhaps using Captain Queeg as an example. Other members might discuss the two or three qualities that each thinks are essential for effective leadership.

Panel members might cite events in which a leader demonstrated specific qualities. (These could include school or community events, such as sports contests or elections; or national and international events, such as the victory of Proposition 13 in California or the negotiation of a peace treaty between Israel and Egypt.) All qualities mentioned should be listed on the chalkboard. After panel members have spoken, the rest of the students should ask questions and present their views. Finally, all students might vote on the five most important qualities they think a good leader should have.

Activities

1. Rules, like laws, have their source in some "government." What government makes the rules for your classroom? For your family? For baseball, football, basketball?

Now suppose there were no rules for your classroom? For your family? For baseball? (You may choose another sport, if you like.) What would happen? Your class might split into three groups, each to prepare an answer to one of those questions. The "answer" may consist of a discussion,

prepared talk, or simulation. In a simulation, a group role-plays (acts out). You might choose a scene which shows a classroom, a family, or a game of baseball without rules. Afterward, be sure to discuss the significance of the "answers."

2. Imagine that tonight *all* government in your community, including all symbols and signs of government, disappears. (Perhaps you can invent a cause for this happening.) Write a short essay or short story describing a day without government in your community.

3. Working individually or in a group, you might write a letter to a Congressional representative discussing how you think the federal government might better carry out one of the main purposes of government as outlined in the Constitution.

4. Some students might make a bulletin-board display, using pictures and headlines cut from old magazines and newspapers, to illustrate the everyday carrying out of each of the six purposes of government.

5. Some utopian communities have espoused the philosophy of anarchy or modifications of it. Some students might find it rewarding to research (perhaps starting with the card catalog in the school or public library) what such communities as Fruitlands and Josiah Warren's Modern Times were like — and what eventually happened to them.

6. Prepare a talk or write a brief essay on this topic: *Are there times when a person has a responsibility to disobey authority?*

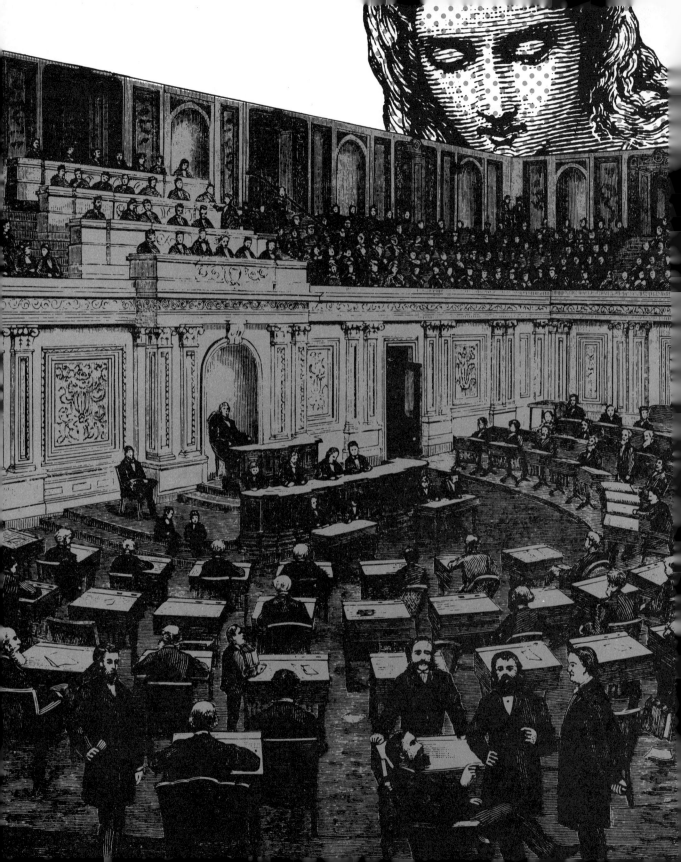

2: HOW TO STUDY GOVERNMENT

Studying government involves more than just reading about it. You also need at least two basic skills. First of all, you should be able to tell the difference between a *value judgment* and a *factual-type statement*.

A value judgment expresses your opinions and feelings. A factual-type statement expresses what you believe to be fact — something that can be proved or disproved.

First skill: the difference between facts and values. Here are three pairs of statements. Each pair consists of a value judgment and a factual-type statement. Can you tell which is which?

Statements about baseball:

A. "Baseball is the most boring sport in the world."

B. "In 1970 Hank Aaron smashed his 715th home run, to break Babe Ruth's record."

Statements about rats:

A. "Rats are hateful, ugly creatures. There should be a worldwide effort to kill them all."

B. "Most mature rats are more than twice as large as most mature mice."

Statements about government:

A. "Bad government is to be feared more than a tiger."

B. "There are more than 87,000 separate government units in the United States, including cities, *counties,** townships, school *districts,** water districts, and so on."

What's the answer? The **A** statement in each pair is a value judgment. The **B** statements are all factual-type statements.

You might argue that Hank Aaron broke Babe Ruth's record in 1974, not 1970. And you'd be right. Nevertheless, this statement is of a factual type. You can prove it to be either right or wrong by doing some research.

But how would you prove the truth or falsehood of statement **A** in the "rats" pair? ("Rats are hateful, ugly creatures. There should be a world-wide effort to kill them all.") You may either agree or disagree with such statements. But your judgment of them would be based on your feelings about rats, not on the facts.

Look again at all three **B** statements. Can you think of a research project that would prove the **B** statements either true or false? Now look at the **A** statements. How would you prove that "bad government" is worse than a tiger? Could you actually prove that baseball is the "most boring sport in the world"?

Why is it so important to know a value judgment when you see one? It is important because *politics** and government can be hot, emotional subjects.

People **who** write and talk about

government often have strong beliefs. They may think that they are telling you the whole truth about *Congress** or *communism** or the Republican party. In fact, they may be telling only their beliefs and feelings. Some people may be swept away into believing all that a writer or speaker tells them. But you will have more control over your own thinking if you can say: "That's a value judgment. Maybe I agree with it. Maybe I don't. But what are the facts?"

This does not mean, of course, that there is anything wrong with expressing value judgments. They are necessary if we are to discuss any important subject. But the more we support our value judgments with facts, the more accurate and helpful they are likely to be.

Second skill: comparing and classifying.

A skill that you'll need for studying government is *classifying.** To understand what classifying means, try this simple exercise. Look over this list of six objects:

- pen;
- pencil;
- paintbrush;
- can of turpentine;
- jar of peanut butter;
- can of sardines.

First, think of a logical way of dividing the objects into *two* piles. The three objects in each pile should have something in common. Second, think of a logical way of sorting the objects into *three* piles. This time there should be two similar objects in each pile. (Your teacher has some suggested answers.)

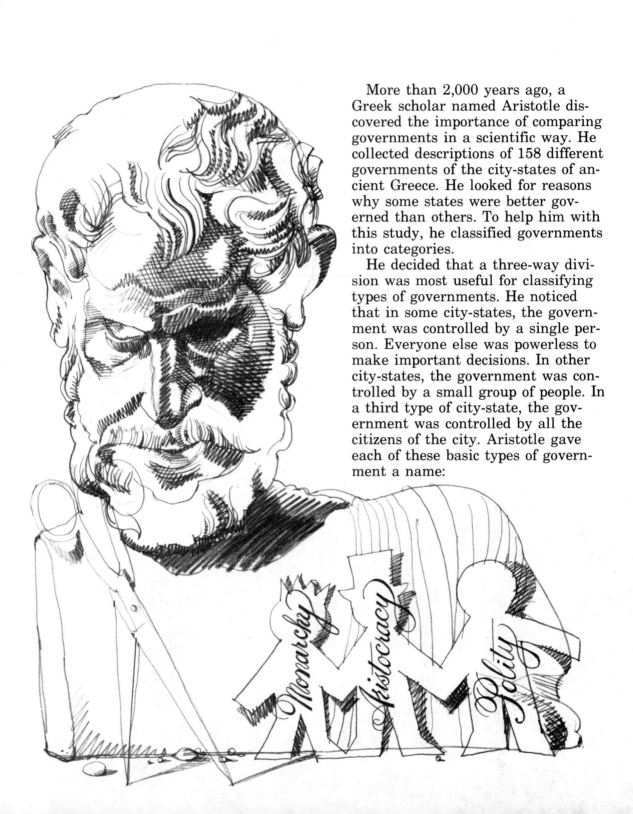

More than 2,000 years ago, a Greek scholar named Aristotle discovered the importance of comparing governments in a scientific way. He collected descriptions of 158 different governments of the city-states of ancient Greece. He looked for reasons why some states were better governed than others. To help him with this study, he classified governments into categories.

He decided that a three-way division was most useful for classifying types of governments. He noticed that in some city-states, the government was controlled by a single person. Everyone else was powerless to make important decisions. In other city-states, the government was controlled by a small group of people. In a third type of city-state, the government was controlled by all the citizens of the city. Aristotle gave each of these basic types of government a name:

Monarchy   Aristocracy   Polity

- rule by one — *monarchy**;
- rule by a few — *aristocracy**;
- rule by many — *polity** or *democracy.**

Types of school government.

You can use Aristotle's classification to figure out how the student government of your school compares with that of other schools. The student governments of five schools are described here.

Three of these student governments are real. Two are made up. See if you can tell which is which. (Your teacher can give you the answers.)

Calhoun Junior High School. The group in charge of student government is called the Student Governing Board (SGB). Most students are between the ages of 12 and 15. But only students over 14 with B averages or better are allowed to take part in SGB elections or activities. This means that only about 10 percent of the students are allowed to vote and hold office. Seven students are elected each year to the SGB. They choose the president. The SGB makes recommendations to the principal on student rules and activities.

Herndon High School. The governing group is called the Student Government Association (SGA). Its officers are elected in schoolwide elections in which all students can vote. The officers are president, vice-president, secretary-treasurer, and historian. The president and vice-president must be members

of the senior or junior classes.

In addition to the four officers, the SGA includes the following elected students: two senators and four class officers from each class (freshman, sophomore, junior, senior); one *representative** from each homeroom.

The SGA discusses such things as dress codes, hall passes, smoking lounges, dances, etc. Its recommendations are usually followed by the school administration.

Hamilton High School. Only seniors approved by a faculty *committee** are eligible to run for president of the Student Government (SG). Usually three or four of these seniors decide to compete for the office. All students may vote in the election for president. The president then has complete power to run the Student Government. He or she appoints other students to help. But there is no board or council to share power with him or her.

Davis High School. The governing body is called the Unified Student Government (USG). The USG is led by the Board of *Regents.** The Board has 13 members. Seven of these are students — chosen in a schoolwide election in which all students can vote. Three members are teachers or other school *personnel** (custodians, staff members) elected by the faculty. The principal and one school board member also attend meetings of the Board of Regents. But they have no vote.

The Board of Regents is advised by four committees. They deal with *budget,** school policy, activities, and

DEMOCRATIC
Rule by the majority through elections. All opposition allowed.

1   **2**   **3**   **4**   **5**

students' rights and responsibilities. These committees, each headed by a member of the Board of Regents, are open to the public as well as students. Anyone who attends two meetings can vote on committee recommendations to the Board of Regents.

The Board of Regents makes decisions — by *majority** vote — on all matters affecting students. If the Board makes a decision, the principal can *veto** it. The Board of Regents can then bypass the principal, if it wishes, and *appeal** directly to the school board.

Sadville Junior High School. One adult has made all student rules in this school for the last 20 years. A few years ago, some teachers and students arranged to have a Student Council elected. Each homeroom could elect one member. At first the Student Council met regularly once a week. But now it seldom meets because members soon learned that they had no power over student rules or activities.

Which school seems to have the most democratic form of government?

(Find the school where power to make rules and decisions is shared by the greatest number of people.)

Which school seems to have an aristocratic form of government? (Find the school or schools where only a small group of people have a role in the government.)

Which school seems to be closest to a monarchy (rule by one)?

Which school has a student government most like your school's?

You may have noticed how hard it is to fit Hamilton High School into *one* of the three kinds of government Aristotle described. You might call it a democracy because all students can vote. But it's also like an aristocracy because only a few students can hold office. And it's also like a monarchy because only one student makes the rules. How do you classify it?

In the next section, we will look at a different way of classifying governments.

Using a scale to compare governments. Before we look at nations which exist today and try to classify their governments, we

34

TOTALITARIAN
Rule by one. No opposition allowed.

6 7 8 9 10

should take another look at the names Aristotle used for "rule by one" (monarchy) and "rule by a few" (aristocracy).

In Aristotle's day a monarchy was ruled by a king or a queen who had almost total power. Today there are so-called monarchies (such as Great Britain) where the king or queen has little power and the "many" rule through elected *officials*.* So *monarchy* is a misleading name today. So is *aristocracy* for "rule by the few." Today when people use the word *aristocracy* they usually mean "upper class*" or "old families."

A more useful word today for both "rule by one" and "rule by a few" is *totalitarianism*.* This term refers to those nations ruled by one person (there are few left today). It also includes nations ruled by a small group (usually leaders of the armed forces or of one *political party*)*.

It can be helpful to try to group items in categories. But it also can be frustrating if you find something — like the Hamilton High School government — that fits into more than one category. Instead of

categories, you might find it more helpful to use a scale like the one above to compare some of today's governments.

In the scale above, **1** stands for the most democratic of governments, and **10** for the most totalitarian. Probably no government today should be rated **1**, for even in the most tolerant democracies, some kinds of opposition are not allowed. (Violent kinds, for example.)

And probably no government today should be rated **10**. For even in the most totalitarian nations, the leader usually shares some power with a small political or military group, and limited criticism (opposition) may be allowed — at least within that group.

The governments of most nations, then, fall somewhere between the democratic extreme of **1** and the totalitarian extreme of **10**.

The governments of four modern nations are described on pages 36–38. After you have read about and discussed them, you might try ranking each on the democratic-totalitarian scale. Then try classifying the U.S. government on the same scale.

**Masayoshi Ohira
Japanese Premier in 1979**

Japan. Like the U.S. Congress, the Japanese *Parliament** is divided into two groups called "houses." The House of Councilors is the upper house, but the *House of Representatives** (or lower house) has more power. Members of both houses are chosen in elections in which everyone over the age of 21 may take part.

The chief executive is the *Prime Minister.** He is chosen by the two houses of Parliament, and is usually the leader of the party that gets the most votes in the parliamentary elections.

The Prime Minister chooses his *Cabinet.** But more than half of the Cabinet officers must be members of Parliament. Most *bills** come from the Cabinet, and they must be approved by Parliament. The Cabinet is the most powerful part of the Japanese government, but it cannot exist without the Parliament. At any time the Parliament may pass a "vote of no confidence" in the Prime Minister and his Cabinet. In that case a new government must be elected.

*Civil rights** are very carefully protected in Japan. The Japanese Constitution *guarantees** 40 different rights, including the right to a job, the right to an education, and the right to speak and write freely.

Israel. Israel's Parliament is called the *Knesset.* It has only one house. All adult Israeli citizens may vote in the elections that choose the members of the Knesset, but citizens do not elect their chief executive, the

Prime Minister, directly. Instead, the Prime Minister is chosen by the Knesset.

There are about a dozen political parties in Israel, each representing different ideas about how the government should be run. The parties cover a wide range of political views, from radical to *conservative.** All are legal, active, and independent. In fact, although the national government is closely tied to the U.S., the city of Nazareth elected a *Communist** mayor in 1975. He was an Arab, which made his election even more unusual.

For the Arabs are a group of people in Israel who might be considered second-class Israelis. If they were born in Israel, they are entitled to be citizens. Like other adult citizens, Arabs can vote, sit in the

36

Knesset, and own businesses. But they may not serve in the army—as other citizens must. Not until 1972 were they allowed to join the Labor party, one of the most powerful political parties in Israel.

Arabs who were not born in Israel but who live there may find it difficult to become citizens. They have legal rights but are sometimes victims of *discrimination** in jobs and education.

South Africa. As in Japan and Israel, South Africa's main *legislative** body is the Parliament. It has two parts — the *Senate** and the House of Representatives. The main job of the Senate is to revise bills that come

**Menachem Begin,
Israeli Prime Minister in 1979**

from the House. The chief executive, or President, is chosen by an *electoral college** which consists of members of Parliament.

Only white adults may become members of Parliament, and only white adults may vote in parliamentary elections. There are four times as many nonwhites as whites in South Africa.

South Africa has a system of laws to keep whites and nonwhites apart. They may not hold the same jobs, live in the same cities, vote in the same elections, or go to the same schools. In fact, while education is compulsory and free for whites, black pupils must pay for school books, examinations, and other items.

While the government allows some (but not much) opposition from whites, it allows almost none from

South African blacks. A person may be put to death for "encouraging hostility toward whites so as to endanger law and order." A black teen-ager received a five-year jail sentence for writing an antiwhite poem and showing it to a girl friend.

One political party has ruled South Africa since 1948.

Paraguay. If you read Paraguay's Constitution, you would think that its government was like the democratic governments of the United States and Western Europe. Paraguay has a President, a *legislature,** and a court system. It has a Constitution that guarantees freedom of speech, the press, and religion.

It has three major political parties — the Colorado, the Liberal, and the Febrerista — and several minor ones. Most Paraguayans vote for their representatives to the national legislature and for their President. Since 1954 one man has won every presidential election. His name is General Alfredo Stroessner.

In reality, the governments of Paraguay and the United States could hardly be more different. For one thing, the Paraguayan Constitution gives the President great power. He appoints all the judges and all the local police chiefs. He commands the army. He makes up the budget. And he can even pass laws when the legislature is not in *session.**

If the President decides that there is an emergency, he may declare a "state of siege." This means that *constitutional** rights may be suspended by the President at any time.

Paraguay has been under a state of siege since 1954. There have been elections since then. But several times General Stroessner has been the only candidate.

There are opposition political parties, but it is risky to join them. In 1974 the leader of the small Christian Democratic party was arrested for the hundredth time. The leader of the Liberal party has been tortured.

There are judges and courts. But "justice" is sometimes carried out in the cells of General Stroessner's secret police. The secret police are called the *pyragues,* meaning "people with hairy feet."

General Alfredo Stroessner, Paraguayan President in 1979

No nation in the world has exactly the same kind of government as any other nation. Each nation has its own special way of choosing officials and making laws. Each has its own system for educating children, *taxing** citizens, and handling people *convicted** of crimes.

For example, there are police and

prisons in both the United States and the Soviet Union. What are the differences between the way American prisoners are treated and the way Soviet prisoners are treated?

Here is an imaginary conversation between a Soviet official, Olga Shmirnov, and an American official, Katy Smith. Let us imagine that they are attending a meeting in Paris on the subject of "Prisons and Justice." Government officials from all nations of the world have been invited to attend the meeting. One morning, after breakfast in a Paris hotel, Katy walks up to Olga and asks if they can talk for a few minutes.

Two students could take the roles of Olga and Katy, and read their conversation aloud. Then all students should be ready to practice the skills learned in this chapter.

Katy: Excuse me. May we talk privately for a minute? I have something I want to show you.

Olga: Yes. What is it?

Katy: It's this book by a wonderful Russian writer. It's all about the prisons in your country. The writer was once a prisoner himself. He therefore knows your system from the inside. (*She takes a paperback book out of her briefcase and shows it to Olga.*)

Olga (*reading the title of the book*): *The Gulag Archipelago* by Solzhenitsyn. Oh yes, I have heard about this terrible book. It is, of course, completely untrue. Don't believe a word of it.

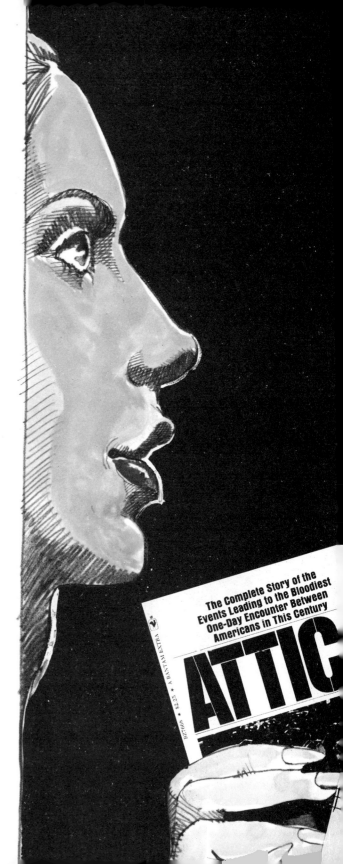

Katy: But have you read it?

Olga: Of course not. The Soviet government would not let the book be published in Russia. Besides, a loyal Russian would not read such a book. Solzhenitsyn is a *traitor*.* We all know that.

Katy: How can you say that? You haven't even read the book. Let me at least read a few lines from it. It can't hurt you, can it?

Olga: All right. I'm listening.

Katy: Here. I've marked the chapter that bothers me the most. It describes 31 methods of torture that he says are commonly used in Russian jails. Thirty-one! The writer says the guards try to force the prisoner to sign a confession saying he committed such-and-such a crime. After that, there may be a phony trial and the poor man or woman is sent away for years to a bleak prison camp. OK, now I'm quoting from page 116 of Solzhenitsyn's book. He's talking about torture treatment number 26.

"Beatings — a kind that leave no marks. They use rubber truncheons, and they use wooden mallets and small sandbags. It is very painful when they hit a bone — for example, a boot kicking the shin, where the bone lies just beneath the skin. They beat Brigade Commander Karpunch-Braven for 21 days in a row. And today he says: 'Even after 30 years all my bones ache — and my head too.' "

In recollecting his own experience and the stories of others, Solzhenitsyn describes many other

tortures. Here is one: "They grip the hand in a special vise so that the prisoner's palm lies flat on the desk — and then they hit the joints with the thin edge of a ruler. And one screams!"

Olga: Very interesting. It sounds very much like the methods used in your country. I was reading last night a book about a prison in the United States. It's called *Attica*. Do you know the book?

Katy: No, but I know about Attica. It's a prison in New York State where prisoners rioted a few years ago. There was a bloody battle and a lot of people were killed, both prisoners and guards. I can't remember how many.

Olga: Yes, the information is right here. (*She takes a book from her briefcase and flips through the pages.*) Yes. Here it is. Thirty-two prisoners were killed and 11 guards. That happened in September 1971. But do you know what happened after the revolt was put down? Allow me to read from page 433 of the official report on Attica.

"One *inmate** described what he saw when he entered a tunnel from the yard. He looked down the tunnel, the inmate remembered, and his legs started to tremble: 'All I saw was *corrections officers** and troopers down both sides of the hallway, and they had clubs in their hands.'

"The tunnel echoed officers' shouts mingled with the bangs of their nightsticks against the brick walls and concrete floor. 'I saw an

41

inmate down on the floor at the end of the tunnel,' the inmate *testified*,* 'just before he got into A block. They were beating him. Another inmate was stopped midway in the tunnel. Then the inmate furthest down in the tunnel was allowed to get up and go into A block; and the inmate in the tunnel started to run. As he ran down, they beat him — whacked him with clubs.' "

I won't read any more. It gets even more disgusting. But you should read this book to know what really happens in your country. This report on Attica was published by a government committee after a long investigation. So it must be true. Here. I'm finished with the book. Take it.

Katy: No, I'm not interested. How can you compare this one case of beating with the horrible and frequent cases of injustice in the U.S.S.R.? In your country, forcing a person to confess is part of the system. It happens almost every day. But in my country, you must be proved guilty in a *jury** trial. There is no such thing as a forced confession.

Olga: Well, I can say the same thing. A Soviet citizen has a right to have his case heard in court. Police beatings and other things of the kind are *illegal** according to Soviet law. And may I say one more thing? Suppose, once in a while, a prisoner is badly treated. I imagine it happens in my country as well as yours. This is just a fact of life. I accept it as such. There is really very little I can do about it.

Katy: I'm sorry. I guess you're really afraid to know the truth about your government. I can understand.

Olga: No, you don't understand. I think you're the one who refuses to see the truth. Good-bye. (*Olga turns on her heel and walks out of the room.*)

Study carefully what both Olga and Katy say about prison conditions in the Soviet Union and the United States. See if you can find three statements from each that you regard as value judgments about treatment of prisoners — and three that you regard as factual-type statements. (You may write these down, or simply note them.)

Next, see how many factual-type statements you can find by Olga or Katy that deal, in any way, with the *sources* of their information about prison conditions in the two countries. (Sources of information are very important, so write these down.)

If you have done your work carefully, you will have discovered an important difference between the way a democratic government and a totalitarian government usually react to charges of official wrongdoing. What is the difference? Which kind of reaction seems to offer the most hope for preventing similar wrongdoing in the future? (Your teacher can give you a summary of the different reactions by the governments.)

"THE LAST WORD"

by Leonid Vladimirov

What makes people loyal to their own system of government? This is one of the common questions asked by scholars who compare governments. These scholars say that every government attempts to train young people to respect and obey its laws. What methods are used for winning a citizen's loyalty?

The reading below is adapted from The Russians, *a book by Leonid Vladimirov. The author wrote for a Soviet newspaper before leaving his country to live in London. In his book, he writes about the Soviet school system.*

There is an old Russian proverb that says you should train a child while he can still lie across the bed. Once he requires the whole bed to lie down on, it is too late to teach him anything. In the Soviet Union, the system of education is based on the wisdom of this proverb.

Children make up a specially favored class of the Soviet state. The younger generation represents the Russia of the future. Therefore the government works hard to make them conform to the Communist *blueprint.** Political training begins early in the nursery school.

The great majority of Russian women work on an equal footing with their husbands. A pregnant woman is given paid leave in her eighth month. This pay continues until two months after her child is born.

Most women go back to work at the end of the period of paid leave. As a result, millions of infants are handed over to the nursery schools. A mother will breast-feed her child in the morning. Then she takes it to a nursery school near her factory or office. At the end of their working day, the women or their husbands collect the children and have them at home until the next morning.

From the second year of their lives, the children in the nursery school are taught to speak, and in some places also to sing and dance.

By the time the child has reached the age of three and is "graduated" from the nursery, he already knows certain things about politics. He will know a number of engaging stories about "Uncle Lenin, who was the nicest man in the whole world." [Lenin led the revolution that created the Soviet government.] He will have learned that "in the old days our country used to be ruled by a wicked *czar.** But then the workers and peasants overthrew him and started to rule the country themselves." He may learn that "the best and cleverest people in our country join the Communist party and are called Communists." By the time he is

44

three, the child also knows about the unbeatable Soviet Army and the glorious frontier troops. They guard the country by night and by day, never letting the enemy cross the borders.

From the ages of three to seven, the young Soviet citizen may attend kindergarten. The young boy or girl gradually acquires what is an extremely important skill in Soviet society. He develops an understanding of which questions one can ask or discuss, and which ones must be avoided. This skill will help him through his life.

In the kindergarten, the staff makes a tremendous effort to make children conform to the group. The teacher may say: "They are all eating porridge, but you are not — shame on you!" "They are all singing the song about the red flag, except you. Are you against all the others?" The greatest *offense** that a child can commit in a Soviet kindergarten is to be different.

(YOU HAVE THE LAST WORD)

In American schools, are children taught to do exactly as other children are doing? Or are they taught, instead, to be independent and speak up for their own ideas? Compare the Russian schools, as described here, with American schools. Are there any important similarities? Any important differences?

An American classroom

45

"CHECKOUT"

Key terms

monarchy	majority	prime minister
aristocracy	totalitarianism	cabinet
democracy	political party	bills
legislature	parliament	

Review

1. Explain the main difference between factual-type statements and value judgments.

2. Name two kinds of factual-type statements and explain how you determine the difference between them.

3. List and define Aristotle's three classifications of governments.

4. List two characteristics each of democratic and totalitarian systems of government.

Discussion

1. As the introduction to The Last Word states, "... scholars who compare governments ... say that every government attempts to train young people to respect and obey its laws." Name as many examples as you can of ways in which governments in our country attempt to do this. List examples on the chalkboard; then discuss their relative effectiveness. Suggest new ways that might be used. Finally, the class might choose, by hand vote, the three most effective.

2. You might set up a panel discussion of your school's student government, focusing on two questions: *How well does it work? In what ways might it be improved?* If there are student government officers or representatives in your class, be sure they are represented on the panel. After panel members have spoken, the chairman should call for questions and comments from the rest of the class.

3. You might enjoy making brief speeches (one minute) to the class in which all statements are either **(a)** value judgments, **(b)** factual-type and true, or **(c)** factual-type and false. Listeners to each presentation should act as critics.

4. "Our country," said Stephen Decatur, "in her intercourse with foreign nations, may she always be right; but our country, right or wrong." "Our country, right or wrong," Carl Schurz said later.

"When right to be kept right; when wrong, to be put right."

Think about these famous statements. Then discuss these questions: *What is loyalty to country? How is it best shown?* After the discussion, see if you can express your feelings about our country in a brief statement beginning, "My country . . ."

5. Explain why the *source* of a value judgement or factual-type statement is important.

Activities

1. Some — or all — of you might choose a different country and read about it in two good updated encyclopedias or in current magazine articles (which you could find by consulting *Reader's Guide to Periodical Literature.*) Afterward, you should rate your respective countries on a 10-point democratic-totalitarian scale. Each rating could be posted on the bulletin board or written on the chalkboard. Each of you should be prepared to explain your rating to the class.

Your teacher may assign different countries. If you choose your own, try to avoid duplication of the choices of other students. An interesting variety of political systems could be found by researching Canada, Mexico, Saudi Arabia, Peru, India, Thailand, Uganda, Chile, West Germany, Egypt, Afghanistan, Taiwan, Poland, Finland, Tanzania, Nigeria, Nicaragua, Sweden, Spain, Singapore, Cuba, Australia.

2. You might invite a visitor to, or an immigrant from, another country to talk about that country's political system, perhaps comparing it to that of the United States. Listen for value judgments and note whether they are supported by factual-type statements. Be sure to ask questions.

3. Watch a 30-minute radio or TV talk show. Jot down especially interesting examples of unsupported value judgments. You might post these on the bulletin board. You might also have a class discussion on the desirability of supporting value judgments with true factual-type statements.

4. Think about the most important cities and towns in your state. Use a state map or atlas to help you. Then classify these towns and cities by population, and in at least two other ways.

5. Think back on your days in kindergarten or elementary school. Compare and contrast your experiences there with those described in The Last Word. Then write a brief biographical essay on the topic: *How my early school days affected my feelings about my country.*

6. Our government is democratic, yet many of the social and economic institutions in it are not (for example, families, the military, businesses). You might list on the chalkboard other institutions in our society which are not democratically run. Then discuss why this is so, and whether it should be so. Students who like to role-play might act out a dinner scene in a family democracy; or a battle-field scene in a military democracy.

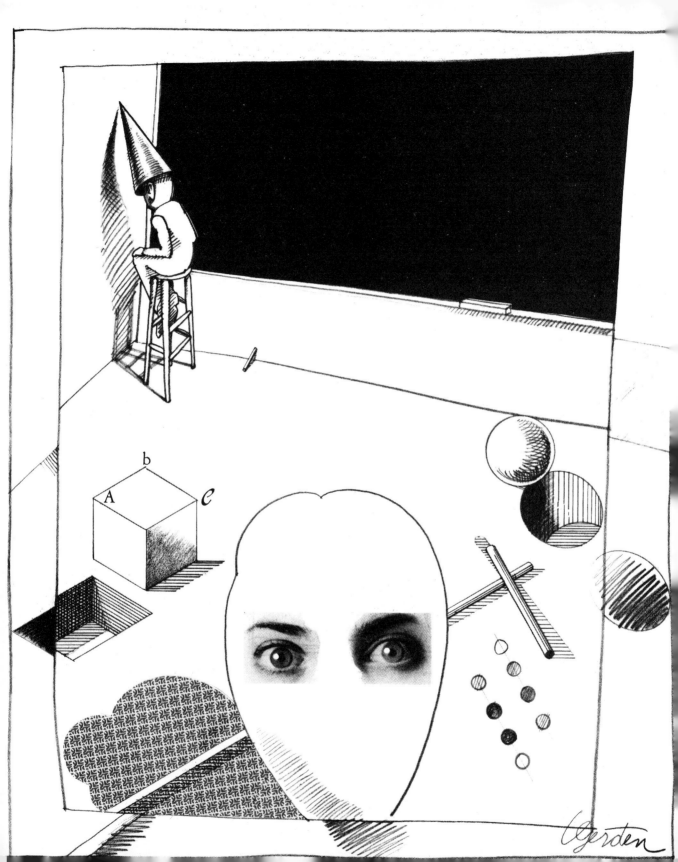

A b c

3: THE DEMOCRATIC IDEA

"Brown-eyed people are more talented than blue-eyed people. They are also more intelligent, as IQ scores show again and again. Do you have brown eyes? Then you belong to a superior group. Do not mix with blue-eyed people. They are weaklings in mind, spirit, and body. But they are also tricky and dangerous. We must fight to keep them in their place. We must always be on our guard against them. Brothers and sisters, let us preserve the purity of our common blood. Be proud of the brown in your eyes. It is the mark of our noble and superior group."

A teacher, Jane Elliott, once made a speech like this to a class of third-graders. For an entire day, students with brown eyes were given special privileges and favors. They sat together in the front of the room while the blue-eyed children all had to sit in back.

Brown-eyed students were always first in line at lunch, first at the fountain, and first out on the playground. They were often praised for

their "outstanding" schoolwork and given high marks. At the same time, spelling mistakes of the blue-eyed children were singled out for criticism. The teacher would ask: "Why are you blue-eyed children so slow? Don't you ever learn anything?"

At the experiment's end, one blue-eyed child described his feelings: "I felt mad," he said, "and I wanted to tie the people with brown eyes up and quit school because they got to do everything first. And we had to do everything last. I felt dirty. And I did not feel as smart as I did before."

Jane Elliott reversed the discrimination the next school day. She wanted her students to know how it felt to be treated as inferiors. She hoped that this would teach them to reject the idea that one group is born superior to another —

or entitled to better treatment.

No nation whose government treats one group of its people as superior — or inferior — to other groups can be truly democratic. Instead, in an ideal democracy, people should all be treated as important and worthy of respect. This is true whether they are born with blue eyes or brown eyes, whether they are rich or poor, male or female, white or nonwhite, young or old.

Many peoples of the world do not think this way. In fact, the democratic idea, as we know it, is rare.

The opposite of democracy.
Look at these photos. The people in both pictures were taught to believe that they were superior beings. The tall African dancers in the first photo are members of the Watusi tribe.

Like many members of their tribe, they are often over seven feet tall. The Watusis think that their unusual height often makes them superior to neighboring tribes in Africa.

Several hundred years ago, Watusi warriors invaded Hutu tribal lands and forced Hutus to work for them and serve them. Even today the Watusi think of the Hutus as an inferior people. They look down upon their former servants — in more ways than one.

Now look at the photo below. It shows German Nazis at a midnight birthday "party" for their leader. The Nazis were a political party that taught its members to hate Jews and other so-called "inferior" groups. Nazi leader Adolf Hitler purposely stirred up feelings of hatred and anger among the German people. Non-Jewish Germans, he said, had superior blood. Therefore they were meant to rule the world. He said in one speech: "I believe today that I am acting the sense of the Almighty Creator. By warding off the Jews I am fighting for the Lord's work."

The Nazis who listened to this man were like the brown-eyed children in Jane Elliott's classroom. However, the speeches the Nazis heard were real ones. And the hatreds were real. *Racism* is the name we give to the ideas preached by Hitler. They are

Adolf Hitler's 50th birthday party

the opposite of democratic ideas.

What is democracy? You now know what democracy is *not*. But what is it? Is it a way of looking at life? Or is it a system of government?

It is both of these things. Each supports the other. First, let's see what democracy means as a *philosophy** of life.

The American patriot, Thomas Jefferson, defined it very simply in five words: "All men are created equal," he wrote in 1776. He probably meant to include women as well as men in this definition. But, to be clear, we should change his statement to read: "All *people* are created equal."

In what way are people created equal? They are not all the same size. Some are stronger than others. Some have better eyesight. Some are smarter.

What then did Jefferson mean? Perhaps he meant that all individuals are worthy of equal respect from the moment of their birth, no matter who they are. In this view, you are equal to every other person in the world because you are born a human being.

But Jefferson might have meant something else. Maybe he meant that any individual *could* be as good as any other, if he or she worked at it. According to this second idea, all people should have an equal chance to make the most of their abilities.

Jefferson never quite explained what he meant by equality. It is a question that you might decide for yourself. But one point is clear: Jefferson *did* mean that all people are entitled to equal treatment by their government.

Abraham Lincoln once defined our democracy in three phrases. He said our government was "of the people, by the people, and for the people." Students of government need to understand what Lincoln meant by each phrase.

Government of the people. The United States government belongs to the American people. The power of ownership and control is what Lincoln means by "government of the people."

For example, who owns the school that you go to? If it's a public school, it's owned by the citizens of your community. The teachers and principal who work in the school are public employees, paid by the taxpayers. The schools are run from day to day by these full-time professionals. But a majority of the people of the town or city can, if they choose, change the way the schools are run.

In a democracy, it is the people who have the final voice and final authority. They "hire" public officials, and they can also "fire" them. They can change the laws because the laws belong to them. They can hire a new state *governor** or a new President for the same reason.

All citizens of a democracy share this power. They may sometimes forget that they have it. They may use it carelessly. Some may not care to use it at all. Still, the power belongs to the people — to you the

52

GOVERNMENT OF THE PEOPLE...

reader, to your teacher, to the author of this book, to every American citizen.

Are you a citizen of the United States? If so, you are automatically the part-owner of billions of dollars worth of property. Your school alone may be worth over a million dollars.

What other public property can you think of that belongs partly to you? Make a list of all the lands and buildings in your town, state, and nation that are partly yours. Can you list 12 public lands and buildings in less than five minutes? What do you think is the total worth of all the properties you've listed?

Of course, there's a catch about property owned by the people as a whole. You, as an individual, can't sell your part and collect money for it. But, nevertheless, you do share in the ownership of all government lands and buildings — and, if you use your rights as a citizen, you can have a voice in their control.

...BY THE PEOPLE...

Government by the people. Many years ago, people made their own candles in their own homes. And, in many places, they also made their own laws.

For example, the citizens of New London, Connecticut, would meet together to discuss a problem. One citizen might say: "The public bridge needs repairing over on the Post Road. How many are in favor of fixing it?" The 50 citizens of the Connecticut village all knew each other. And they knew the problem. Governing the town was a simple matter of counting hands.

"All in favor, raise your right hand," the leader of the meeting might say. Then he would count the hands. Next he would count those opposed to repairing the bridge. A majority of hands would decide whether the bridge got fixed or not.

Such a system is known as "direct" democracy — because the citizens themselves run the government directly. In the United States today, direct democracy is probably not possible. Imagine 230 million Americans trying to meet together once a week to discuss public business. Think of the parking problem alone!

Instead of direct "government by the people," the U.S. has "government

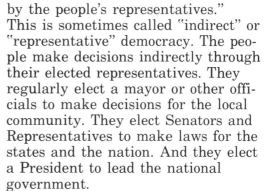

by the people's representatives." This is sometimes called "indirect" or "representative" democracy. The people make decisions indirectly through their elected representatives. They regularly elect a mayor or other officials to make decisions for the local community. They elect Senators and Representatives to make laws for the states and the nation. And they elect a President to lead the national government.

In a representative system of democracy, there is always the question: How should the representatives be chosen?

Suppose, for example, your school could send three representatives to a national meeting to discuss ways of improving education. Here are three possible plans for choosing representatives:

Plan A. Female students elect one female representative. Male students elect one male representative. Teachers elect one teacher representative.

Plan B. All teachers and students in the school vote for all three representatives who can be from any of the groups.

Plan C. All students elect two representatives. Teachers elect one.

Which plan seems to best fit "government by the people"? Why? Can you think of a better plan for representing your school in this national meeting? If so, what is it?

Government for the people. In a democracy, government is supposed to serve all the people — not just favored groups, as in some countries.

55

The United States is a nation of many thousands of different groups. We are Protestants, Catholics, Jews, nonbelievers, etc. We are Mexican Americans, Italian Americans, Anglo Americans, Afro Americans, Japanese Americans, etc. We are factory workers, teachers, farmers, clerks, singers, shop owners, etc. We are young, old, middle-aged.

There are laws that benefit oil companies and other laws that benefit poor people, workers, nature lovers. Some laws help women to get better jobs; others help different groups. It's true that business people have an influence on government. But so do labor *unions** — and thousands of other groups that make up America.

Democratic government at its best works for all the people, including you. That is what Lincoln meant by "government for the people."

Now let's look at one way our democratic government can help you to enjoy a better life. One of the most important functions of a democratic government is to help its citizens learn skills that can both give them satisfaction and be useful to society. On a sheet of paper, copy the following sentence:

"I could enjoy life more if I learned how to be a great _____." Fill in the last word (or words) of the sentence. Examples of words you might use: cook, athlete, singer, typist, talker, teacher, driver, actor, photographer, mechanic, deep-sea diver, friend, parent. Be able to explain your choice.

...FOR THE PEOPLE

members of the class). The money can be spent for any purpose that your chosen representatives agree upon. Your representatives can decide to buy a car, throw a party, put the money in a bank, donate the money to a worthy cause — anything at all.

But the people's representatives — the elected lawmakers of the class — must make the final decision. How shall the representatives be chosen? The class might divide into four groups of roughly equal size. Each small group then chooses one person to represent it in the government.

Next, each small group, including its representative, discusses what should be done with the $1,000. They might spend five or 10 minutes discussing ideas until they all agree upon a single plan. If all cannot agree, then the group should vote. Of course, the majority rules.

Then the representatives meet together in the front of the room. Each presents the plan of his or her group. Are all plans the same? If not, the representatives may change their plans to satisfy the others. The money can be spent "for the people" only if at least three of the representatives agree upon a single plan.

A representative may go back to talk with members of his or her group at any time.

How long does it take for people to agree on a common plan? What does this activity suggest about democratic government? Is it easy or hard to make the decision the democratic way?

Democratic government may sound like a fairly simple idea. What could be easier than government of the people, by the people, and for the people? Democracy would be easy if everyone agreed on what the government should do for people. But do people often agree about what should be done?

You might find out by pretending that your class is a group governed in a democratic way. All members of the class have equal power. They have an equal share in deciding what the government should do for them.

Suppose that this government has $1,000 to spend for the "people" (all

"THE LAST WORD"

by Studs Terkel

How many American citizens sincerely believe in democracy and practice it in their daily lives? A radio announcer, Studs Terkel, interviewed 70 people from a neighborhood in Chicago. He later wrote Division Street: America, *a book containing those people's thoughts about life. The passage below is adapted from that book. It gives the thoughts of Dennis Hart, a cab driver.*

You have to feel something for people. There was a time in my early 20's, I'd see people bleed, I'd see people cry. I didn't feel anything. I began to hate myself. Now I feel I've conquered this. Crying with this man when he's been hit, I feel the punch. It keeps you young.

I think really what changed me was working as a guard in the county jail. So many of the things are so unnecessary. You hear the train whistle coming through at three in the morning. Why are these guys here? They're so young. One fella said, "What time is it?" And I said, "Why? Are you gonna catch a plane or something?" After I said it, after I made the punch on the clock, I realized I made a fool of myself.

I went back and I actually apologized to this guy in a round-about way. A guard is not supposed to give in in any way whatsoever. You're supposed to stay above these guys. But I felt terrible. I think it was the human thing to do.

As I sat down, I had to think of a way to apologize. I didn't come out and say to this man, "I'm sorry for what I said." But I went back and paid a little more attention to him and he understood that I was sorry and I felt I was forgiven.

(YOU HAVE THE LAST WORD)

In a democracy, who is entitled to be treated by the government as your equal? **(a)** The governor of your state. **(b)** Someone on *welfare.** **(c)** A school dropout. **(d)** A retarded child. **(e)** A wino. **(f)** A convicted murderer. Explain your answers.

Would you say Dennis Hart believes in democracy? Why or why not?

"CHECKOUT"

Key terms
discrimination
racism
equality

direct democracy
representative democracy

Review

1. Who has the final authority in a democracy?

2. Explain — using one sentence for each phrase — what is meant by "government of the people, by the people, and for the people."

3. Explain the difference between direct democracy and representative (or indirect) democracy.

4. Explain at least three ways of interpreting the statement: *All men are created equal.*

Discussion

1. Winston Churchill said: *Democracy is the worst form of government — except for all the others.* What do you think he meant? Think about that. Then list on the chalkboard strengths and weaknesses of democratic political systems. (For example: *Strength:* People elect their leaders; *Weakness:* Many people don't bother to vote.) Next list strengths and weaknesses of nondemocratic political systems. (For example: *Strength:* There are no unruly demonstrations against the government; *Weakness:* There is no free speech.)

After your class has listed as many specific strengths and weaknesses of democratic and nondemocratic systems as you can think of in 10 or 12 minutes, see if you can summarize each list in a few words or phrases. After further discussion, the class as a whole might decide whether they agree or disagree with Churchill's statement.

2. You might name different groups of people in our country who have been discriminated against in the past and the present. Write their names on the chalkboard. Then discuss these questions: *How many of the groups have obvious physical differences? Why is this often the basis for discrimination?*

3. Think about how modern technology *might* make it possible to have nationwide direct democracy. It has been suggested that two-way cable TV could allow people to discuss issues and register their votes after hearing the issues debated. Would this be a good idea? Why or why not?

60

4. *Governments and laws alone cannot create or sustain a democratic society. Perhaps equally important are the attitudes of the majority of people toward their government, and toward their fellow citizens.* Do you agree with this view? Why or why not?

Activities

1. Students might volunteer to research and report on the consequences of Hitler's racial policies — the holocaust. Making use of *Reader's Guide* (for magazine articles), and the card catalog in the local or public library (for books), researchers could find an abundance of information on the various concentration camps where Jews — and other groups the Nazis judged "inferior" — were killed. One student might focus on Auschwitz, another on Majdanek, and so on. (Other important camps were Buchenwald, Dachau, Belsen, and Treblinka.)

After the reports, the class might discuss the following: *Hitler came to power in a democracy, in one of the best-educated nations in the world. How can our democracy best protect itself against would-be führers?*

2. According to the text, "One of the most important functions of a democratic government is to help its citizens learn skills that can both give them satisfaction and be useful to society." Then you are asked to complete this sentence: "I could enjoy life more if I learned how to be a great _____." After you have completed the sentence, think about and list the ways you think governments might help — or hinder — the realization of your ambition.

3. Students might prepare a bulletin board display titled "The Democratic Idea," with pictures, drawings, headlines, and articles illustrating democracy in action.

4. You might create a questionnaire like this: *Which of the following statements best describes equality, as you understand it?*

(a) *Equality means that all people are entitled to equal respect.*

(b) *Equality means that all people should have an equal chance to make the most of their abilities.*

(c) *Equality means that all people are entitled to equal treatment by their government.*

(d) *Equality means that the government has a responsibility to help the disadvantaged catch up with those who have had greater opportunities.*

Then, using the questionnaire, you might poll people in your school or community. The results could be recorded on the chalkboard and their significance discussed in class.

5. An experiment like Jane Elliott's might be tried in your class. Afterward, discuss your reactions.

6. *Is democracy gaining — or losing — in our world today?* Some of you might volunteer to research this question, investigating recent changes in such countries as India, Spain, Portugal — and reporting new changes as they occur in countries throughout the world. Others might sketch maps of the world for posting, showing democratic and totalitarian countries in distinctive colors.

EIGHT GOOD BOOKS ABOUT DEMOCRATS AND DICTATORS

Brave New World

by Aldous Huxley

"Going to the feelies this evening, Henry?" As you'll discover in this book, a feelie is one of the ways people of the future may amuse themselves. Like everything else in this future world, feelies are created by the government to keep people happy. The author of this famous book of science fiction fears that our daily lives may someday be run by the government. Can this ever happen? Is it happening now? Harper & Row, New York, 1932.

A Dangerous Freedom

by Bradford Smith

This is a collection of stories showing what Americans have done to keep their democracy alive. Do you doubt that the American people really run the government? This book will give you hope about the power of the people to run their own lives and their own government. J.B. Lippincott, Philadelphia, 1952.

Division Street: America

by Studs Terkel

This is a book about people who

seldom make headlines in the newspapers. Police officers, sales clerks, teachers talk about their ambitions and problems. A hot-dog vendor tells why he cheats people out of their money. Americans who are white, black, Indian, Mexican, rich, poor, and middle class all express their ideas about living in a democracy. Read the stories of any 10 of these people. Then ask yourself again: Are all people created equal? Are all Americans equally democratic? Pantheon, New York, 1967.

Gandhi: Fighter Without a Sword
by Jeanette Eaton
This book tells the life story of a great democrat who led the *nonviolent** struggle to free India from British control. He hated to see one person mistreated by another. His love for human beings of all colors and religions proved stronger than British armies, jails, and unjust laws. William Morrow, New York, 1950.

Lord of the Flies
by William Golding
Imagine that you and a group of friends are stranded on an island. The island is inhabited by wild hogs, but by no other human beings. Could you find a way to survive? Would you need someone to lead the group? Should this leader act in a democratic way — or like a *dictator**? Find out what the author thinks would happen to you. Coward, McCann & Geoghegan, New York, 1962.

Nicholas and Alexandra
by Robert K. Massie
Not so long ago, most nations of the world were ruled by monarchs. Russia's monarch was called a czar. Like all governments, a czar's government was supposed to look out for people's welfare and to protect the country from dangers of all kinds. What happens if a czar is kind and well-meaning — but weak? Find out by reading this interesting book. It's better than the movie that was made from it. Atheneum, New York, 1967.

The Night of the Long Knives
by Max Gallo
"In Munich, as in Berlin, the killers are at work." This is not fiction; it is real and also horrifying. The book tells what happened in Germany in 1934 when Adolf Hitler decided to get rid of the gang leaders who had helped place him in power. As you read this thriller, you'll learn about the methods of one of the most brutal dictators in world history. Harper & Row, New York, 1972.

Winning Is the Only Thing
by Jerry Kramer, Editor
Like all groups, a football team needs a government too. Vince Lombardi, former coach of the Green Bay Packers, gave his teams the kind of leadership that won championships — but not everyone approved of his methods. Read what the people who played for him said about his leadership. Then decide whether Lombardi should be called a democrat — or a dictator. World, New York, 1970.

UNIT II: WRITING THE CONSTITUTION

4: HOW DO YOU REACT TO TYRANNY?

Imagine that you are living in the year 1995. You are now nearing middle age. A great deal has happened in the world since the days long ago when you were a teenager in school. For one thing, the U.S. government has begun to act in strange new ways.

On every block in your community, there are citizens who have been made into government agents. These Deputy Eagles, as they are called, wear bright orange uniforms with a blue eagle on the right sleeve. Deputy Eagles are supposed to be tough and ruthless. Their job is to carry out commands from Eagle headquarters in Washington, D.C.

In the last week, three things have happened to your neighborhood that have caused you to think long and hard about your government.

Monday morning. A Deputy Eagle knocked on your door and asked to see your TV set. "What for?" you wanted to know. He said he had orders to put a tax meter on the set. From now on, he explained, the act of watching TV would be taxed at the rate of five dollars an hour. You told him to come back another time. But he barged right in anyway and placed a tax meter on every one of your three TV sets.

Thursday afternoon. Your next-door neighbors, Martha and Max Pearson, warned you to be prepared for another visit from the Deputy Eagles. The Pearsons were told that the government intends to use their guest room for two Deputy Eagles from out-of-state. The government is holding a *convention** of 100,000 Deputy Eagles in your community and every homeowner must give one or two Eagles room and board for a week. Martha Pearson was furious about it.

Sunday night. A midnight call from Max Pearson got you out of bed. "They've taken Martha!" Max shouted. "They've taken her away! They just came in and took her!" After much trouble calming Max down, you learned that two Eagles had broken into the Pearson house, seized Martha, and carried her off. They said they were taking her to Washington for questioning.

You're almost as shocked as Max is. Martha always seemed like such a nice, harmless person. But now you suspect that Martha may be a rebel against the U.S. government. Why else would the Eagles have arrested her?

You're greatly disturbed by these three events. But you're unsure what to do. You have a number of choices:

1. Do and say nothing.

2. Send a letter of complaint to Eagle headquarters in Washington and demand an explanation for Martha's arrest.

3. Wait until the next election when you can help to elect a new President or a new Congress. (Unfortunately, the President and Congress now take orders from the Eagles.)

4. Become a rebel and risk your life for the cause of American freedom.

Are there any other choices that you can think of? What do you think you would probably do if, in 1995, the government taxed your TV, commanded the use of your house, and arrested your neighbor for some unknown crime?

Revolt against tyranny, 1776. Your imaginary troubles with the Deputy Eagles of 1995 are much like the real troubles of American colonists 200 years ago. In those days, America was part of the British *Empire.** Most young Americans growing up in the 1750's felt loyal to the King of England. But that was before the British government tried to meddle in people's everyday lives.

In 1765, instead of placing tax meters on TV sets, the British government appointed tax agents to collect *stamp taxes** on newspapers, pamphlets, and legal papers. Instead of being required to feed and house Deputy Eagles, the citizens of Boston were forced to give lodging to British soldiers or *redcoats.**

In those days it was common to hear people talk angrily about something they called *tyranny.** They were sure that an evil ruler or *tyrant** could make slaves of them

of the STAMP

An Emblem of the Effects

O! the fatal Stamp

unless they stood up for their rights. Many Americans decided that they would rather be outlaws and rebels than be turned into slaves by a British king who they thought was a tyrant.

Therefore, instead of paying the new stamp tax of 1765, the colonists sent threatening letters to the king's tax collectors. They drove the collectors out of their houses, stripped off their coats and trousers, and covered their bodies with hot, sticky tar and feathers.

In Boston, the citizens learned to hate the British soldiers who had been sent to their city to keep order. One chilly day in March 1770, a street mob surrounded a group of soldiers and pelted them with snowballs, sticks, and oyster shells. The soldiers lost patience and fired into the crowd, killing five Americans.

This Boston *Massacre,** as it was called, stirred up more talk of British tyranny. "It is high time," wrote one citizen, "for the people of this country to declare whether they will be free men or slaves."

Finally, a group of Americans,

meeting in Philadelphia in 1776, decided that they could stand the tyranny no longer. They would fight and perhaps die, rather than submit. A young Virginian named Thomas Jefferson was given the job of writing a "Declaration of Independence" for America. Jefferson listed many acts of the English king, George III, to try to prove that the king was a tyrant. These were some of the charges:

"He has kept among us, in times of peace, standing armies without the consent of our legislatures. . . . He has plundered our seas, ravaged our coasts, burned our towns, and destroyed the lives of our people." (See pages 795–797 for other charges against George III.)

Fifty-six *delegates** from the 13 American colonies signed the Declaration of Independence. Dipping a quill pen in a bottle of ink, each signer realized that he could be "hanged by the neck until dead" for this act of *treason** against the British Empire.

The beginnings of American government. As it turned out, none of the signers of the Declaration was hanged. After eight years of fighting American armies led by George Washington, the British gave up the struggle in 1783.

But the American form of government really did not begin in 1783 or 1776. Our ideas about liberty, tyranny, and the rights of people go back hundreds of years. We can trace the beginnings of American government as far back as the year 1215

Colonists tar and feather a British tax collector

We hold these

— 200 years before Christopher Columbus was even born.

In 1215 King John of England, who had used brutal methods against his enemies, was forced to recognize the rights of free citizens. A group of nobles threatened him with open revolt unless he promised never again to misuse his power in certain ways.

The king, after much fuss and fury, agreed to put his seal to a piece of parchment called the *Magna Charta** (Great Charter). The Magna Charta listed his promises to the English people. And from 1215 on it was used to remind kings that free citizens had rights which even a king could not ignore. A citizen could not, for example, be kept in prison without first being judged by a jury of his fellow citizens.

The British people continued to struggle with their kings. Over the years, they won new rights and liberties — new guarantees against cruel and unfair actions by government officials.

Because of those struggles, the British who later settled in the colonies of America brought with them a firm belief in their rights. As you'll see later, they insisted that these rights become part of the Constitution of the new United States government.

There was a second idea about government that also had a long history in the American colonies. That was the idea that the common people were intelligent enough to run their own government and make their own laws.

The settlers who first came to Virginia, Pennsylvania, and Massachusetts quickly set up governments of their own. They had no other choice. They could not depend on the British government to make decisions for them. After all, it took a ship six weeks of good sailing weather to deliver a message from the colonies to England. It took another six weeks to get an answer back. The colonists could not wait that long for an answer to their problems. To survive in the wilderness, they had to rely on themselves and their own judgment of what laws were needed.

British officials appointed governors for most of the colonies to enforce the laws of England. But often these laws, because they were made so far away, seemed to make no sense to the colonists in America. The laws that made sense were those that the Americans made themselves in their own lawmaking bodies, called *assemblies.**

They complained of tyranny whenever the king's governor tried to make policy without the approval of the assembly. After a while, the colonists began to believe that no laws could be fair or right unless they had "the consent of the people." And how do people either give their consent or refuse to give it? Through the majority vote of their elected representatives meeting in assembly.

"We hold these truths. . . ."

What were people celebrating on July 4, 1776, when the Declaration of Independence was read aloud to crowds

71

of joyous Americans? They were re-
joicing in the thought that they were
part of a great new nation. This nation would be ruled, not by kings and
wealthy lords, but by the people
themselves. Unlike any other nation
in the world, this new nation would
have a government based on the
following two ideas:

• that individuals have rights which
governments cannot trample;

• that all laws must have the
consent of the governed.

Both of these ideas are expressed
most beautifully in a famous passage
of the Declaration of Independence.
You read part of it in Chapter 1.
But it is so important to an understanding of the basic ideals of our
government that it is worth reading
again — in full:

"We hold these truths to be self-
evident, that all men are created
equal, that they are endowed by their
Creator with certain unalienable
rights, that among these are life, liberty, and the pursuit of happiness.
That to secure these rights, governments are instituted among men,
deriving their just powers from the
consent of the governed."

The rights of free citizens. "Give
me liberty or give me death!" Patrick
Henry, a citizen of Virginia, once
said this in one of the most famous
speeches of all time. What did he
mean by it? Henry believed that the
time had come to fight and perhaps
die for his rights as a free citizen. Do
you feel as strongly about these
rights as Patrick Henry did?

Here is a list of five of the rights
that Henry and other Americans
were willing to fight for in 1776.
How important are these rights to
you? Ask yourself if each right is:

• so important you would rather
fight than have the right taken away
from you;

• very important, but you wouldn't
fight to protect it;

• important, but you could easily
live without it;

• unimportant — you wouldn't miss
it at all.

First right. The right to a trial by
jury. This right protects
you from government
officials' arresting you
and putting you in jail
without giving you

a fair chance to defend yourself.

Second right. The right to be taxed only by your own elected representatives. This right gives you some control over the taxes you pay to the government. Without this right, you would be at the mercy of lawmakers and tax collectors who might not care about your needs.

Third right. The right to be safe from cruel and unusual punishments. Without this right, citizens could be tortured or put to death for any crime.

Fourth right. The right to be safe from the unlawful search of your house and property. Without this right, government officials could break into your house at any time for any reason.

Patrick Henry

Fifth right. The right to print all kinds of opinions in newpapers — even opinions that criticize government officials. Without this right, newspapers could print only those stories and editorial opinions that the government approved.

These were only some of the rights that many Americans of 1776 said they would fight and die for, if necessary. They believed that the King of England and his ministers had tried to take from Americans every one of these rights. The Declaration of Independence listed more than 20 ways that King George III was trying to stamp out people's rights.

Therefore, said the Declaration, the American people had a *duty* to fight and overthrow the British government. Do you agree with this idea? Do people have a duty, even today, to fight if necessary for the five rights listed here? Suppose that the first and second rights were taken from only 1,000 Americans. Would this be enough to make you fight?

Who should be allowed to govern? Every signer of the Declaration of Independence was sure that *his* rights were important enough to fight for.

But when the Constitution was written 11 years later, the *Founding Fathers** were less sure about another question. Could all adult Americans be trusted to govern themselves wisely and well? Many of those who created the Constitution did not think so.

They thought that only the best-educated citizens could be trusted to make good laws and wise decisions. Other people, they thought, did not know enough to hold office or even to vote. A list follows of five groups of Americans who lived in 1787. Which of these groups was best qualified to run the government of a new country? Which was least qualified? Would you have allowed all of these groups an equal voice in voting and making laws? Or would you have allowed only the "best-qualified" people to vote and hold office?

Group A. Wealthy merchants, lawyers, planters, and doctors. Members of this group were better educated than most college graduates are today. Most of them had traveled a great deal. Most were well informed about both business and politics. Many had their own private libraries and were constantly reading books on serious subjects.

Group B. Farmers, craftsmen, ministers, and small shopkeepers. Members of this group owned a small amount of land and property. Most of the ministers had been to college. The others had probably had a few years of basic education and knew how to read and write. Many read newspapers regularly, as well as some books and pamphlets.

Group C. Unskilled laborers. Members of this group might not have gone to school. Many of them could not write their own names. They did most of the hard labor — digging, hauling goods, and loading

ships. They worked for low wages. Some were so poor that they slept in the streets and fields.

Group D. African slaves. Members of this group worked for people in groups A and B. Some were born into slavery. Others had recently arrived from Africa. In the tribes from which they came, some were leaders. But here they were bought, sold, whipped, and made to work in the same way that horses or cattle were treated. Slaves had no rights as human beings. Few could either read or write.

Group E. Women. Members of this group also belonged to each of the other four groups. Many of the wealthier women were as well educated as the men. But they had almost no experience in politics and govern-ment. The men who made the laws had so far prevented them from voting or holding office.

The people who wrote the Constitution were all from groups A and B. They felt confident that men in these two groups could govern the new nation. They believed that the citizens of this nation would have more freedom than any other people in history.

And they had reason to believe this. In 1787 no nation in the world had as many men who could call themselves truly free. Until that time, no nation was based on the idea that a citizen's rights were as important as life itself.

Later in this book, you'll see how this idea spread until all groups were given equal rights.

When should you be loyal to the established government of your country? And when should you be prepared to rebel against it?

That was the question that troubled Americans back in 1776. Some citizens found it easier than others to rebel against British tyranny. Even after American independence was declared in Philadelphia, many Americans still felt loyal to the British government. Members of the same family often ended up fighting each other in the American Revolution. For example, Benjamin Franklin helped to write the Declaration of Independence. But his own son, William Franklin, remained loyal to the British.

How do people react to tyranny? It all depends on the person. Some people, like Patrick Henry, have a hot temper. They are the first to shout: "Give me liberty or give me death!" It takes a lot longer for others to be aroused by *evidence** of injustice and tyranny. Still others so dislike the idea of rebelling that they remain "loyal" no matter what happens.

How would *you* react to tyranny? How would you react to the imaginary events listed below? When, if ever, would you join a rebellion against the Deputy Eagles? Let us suppose that the rebel group calls itself the SDL (Sons and Daughters of Liberty). In what year — if ever — would you join such a group?

1995. Deputy Eagles place tax meters on your TV sets. Your neighbor, Martha Pearson, is arrested, probably because of her membership in the SDL.

1997. Your newspaper reports that Martha Pearson has been kept in jail for two years without a trial. It says the government has tried to force her to sign a confession of her "crime."

1998. The editor of your newspaper is arrested for printing "disloyal and untrue" statements. Twenty-five editors of other newspapers are also arrested for the same reason.

1999. An angry group of citizens gathers outside Martha Pearson's prison. They demand that Martha be released. Deputy Eagles shoot into the crowd, killing 10 people.

2000. The Chief of the Deputy Eagles makes a TV speech declaring that the SDL is plotting to overthrow the U.S. government. Anyone in the SDL shall therefore lose all rights of citizenship.

2001. A bomb explodes in Deputy

Eagle headquarters, killing five officers. Government officials blame the SDL and arrest 10,000 people. Among them is your sister.

2002. The Chief of the Deputy Eagles declares a state of emergency. Fifty leaders of the SDL are sentenced to be shot by a firing squad. The execution is shown on TV to teach other citizens a lesson.

2004. The election of the President and of Congress is called off. The Deputy Eagles declare that there shall be no more elections until all traitors are caught and punished. Until then, all laws will be made by the Chief. And Congress shall not be allowed to meet.

Have you joined the rebel group yet? Have your classmates?

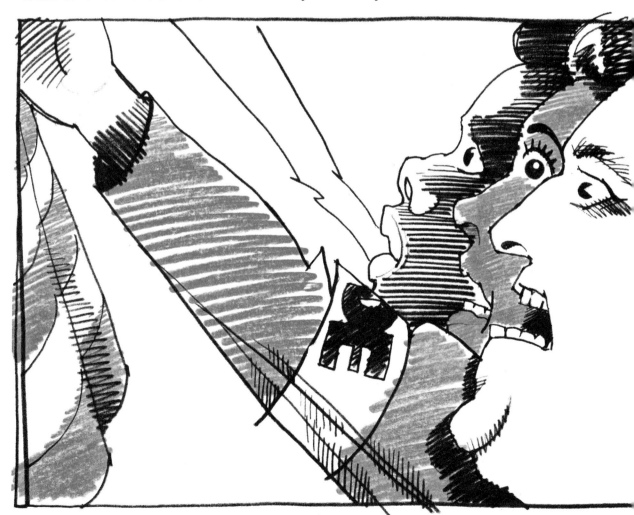

"THE LAST WORD"

by Howard Fast

You may have heard of the "shot heard round the world." It was fired early one April morning in 1775, as British soldiers marched down a country road that led through Lexington, Massachusetts. A novel by Howard Fast, April Morning, *gives us a vivid idea of how the citizens of Lexington reacted to the news of the British march. The story is told from the point of view of a 15-year-old youth whose father, Moses Cooper, is one of the town leaders. The passage below is adapted from the novel. In it, everyone in town is out on the Lexington Green debating what to do. The minister or "Reverend" argues that nothing can be done.*

"The point I want to make," the Reverend said, "is this. Just for the sake of argument, suppose there is an army of a thousand men bound this way. Now that puts the question up to us, doesn't it? The *muster roll** of the committee adds up to 79 men — providing nobody's sick or absent.

"Now it's all very well to talk about our rights. But just what are we going to do with 79 men facing a thousand? Good heavens, brothers, it's not like we had experience in this line of work. We are not soldiers. The only man in my congregation who ever shot another is poor Israel Smith, when he put a load of bird shot into his brother Joash's sitting place. And I see Joash standing there, and he'll tell you it's not a rewarding experience, not for him who gives or for him who receives."

"I say amen to that," Joash Smith agreed.

If he had only put it a little differently, the Reverend would have had my father on his side. But when the Reverend came straight out with his doubts concerning the odds, 79 to a thousand, my father had to object.

"Reverend," he said, "with all deference to your experience as a *man of the cloth,** you seem to have missed the point."

"How?" the Reverend demanded.

"You have forgotten about our duty! Our oath in the holy name of freedom!" Father cracked out the words like a dead shot. "Is our *principle** flexible? Have we drilled a *militia** only to sweep it into hiding at the first glimpse of a thieving redcoat?"

Father was taken. He could never resist the sound of his own words. And when he saw that the crowd was with him, he just couldn't bear to stop. "I say no! I say that right and justice are on our side! Who are these red-coated bandits that we should fear them? We know where they find their so-called soldiers.

78

They are the sweepings of the filthy alleys of London, the population of their jails, the men condemned to the gallows and reprieved to teach us legality! We know them, and we fear them not! Our course remains the just cause!"

I felt like jumping up and cheering. It was as good as the best the Reverend had ever done on hell-fire and damnation. And it made my skin prickle and my hair stand on end just to listen.When the crowd let out a whoop, I whooped with the best of them. I was just as proud as punch.

Yet I think the Reverend's face was sad, and for some reason the fire went out of him. It wasn't like him to step down from a hot issue. But this time he did. He just nodded.

"I'm going to muster the militia, by God. I'm going to!" Jonas Parker cried.

"Can we have the bells, Reverend?" Cousin Simmons asked him.

He just nodded again, and half a dozen of the boys, myself among them, raced for the church, to have a hand in the ringing of the bells.

(YOU HAVE THE LAST WORD)

You know how this story ends. Inspired by Moses Cooper's words the Minutemen line up at Lexington Green without really meaning to start a fight. The British soldiers open fire on them, killing Moses Cooper and six others. After this event, war and revolution cannot be avoided.

But now imagine what might have happened if the Reverend had won the argument. No militia on Lexington Green on that morning in 1775. No deaths. And possibly no war. Do you prefer this more peaceful ending to history? Do you think we would still be British subjects if Americans had failed to make a stand on Lexington Green in 1775?

Battle of Lexington

"CHECKOUT"

Key terms

British empire	Boston Massacre	treason
stamp taxes	delegates	Magna Charta
tyranny	Declaration of Independence	

Review

1. Give two examples of what the American colonists considered tyranny by the British government.

2. List two ideas on which the Declaration of Independence is based.

3. List five rights for which the American Revolution was fought.

4. Name the classes of people who were allowed to vote in the earliest period of the U.S. government.

5. What right protects you from being jailed without a chance to defend yourself?

Discussion

1. If one group of people in a country has the rights for which the American Revolution was fought, do these people have a duty to make sure that other people have them? Why or why not? If there is such a duty, discuss ways in which average citizens — including young people — can help fulfill it.

2. Your class might have a panel discussion led by students who have read George Orwell's *1984,* Sinclair Lewis' *It Can't Happen Here,* or Aldous Huxley's *Brave New World.* The discussion would focus on the question: *How do these authors think people react to tyranny?*

Afterward, students would have an opportunity to express their own views on a related topic: *How do you think Americans would react if a dictator took over our government and denied us our basic rights?*

3. Imagine it is July 1776, and you have been celebrating the news that independence has been declared. When you reach home, your Tory neighbor — a colonist loyal to the king — asks why you're celebrating. What would you say to him? What do you imagine he might say to you?

Activities

1. "We hold these truths to be self-evident, that all men ... are endowed by their Creator with certain unalienable rights...." For most people living in the world in 1776 — and for many today — such "truths" were, and are not, "self-evident." Where did Jefferson, who wrote these words, and other signers of the Declaration of Independence who approved them, get the idea of "unalienable rights"? You might volunteer to research this question and report your findings to the class. You could begin by looking up these topics and names in a good encyclopedia: *Declaration of Independence, natural rights, Thomas Jefferson, John Locke.* You might also refer to Gary Wills' 1978 study, *Inventing America: Jefferson's Declaration of Independence.*

2. Students might volunteer to watch newspapers and clip articles about independence movements all over the world. Other students might clip articles about situations in which people are denied their "unalienable rights." Both sets of clippings could be posted on the bulletin board under appropriate headings.

3. You might invite a speaker who has lived in a former colony to talk about how his or her country achieved independence.

4. A volunteer might check the library for a recording of the musical *1776* and choose appropriate selections to play in class. Other students might obtain copies of the play and act out an appropriate scene in class.

5. The people in the Canadian colonies did not revolt in 1776. In 1980 Canada, although a sovereign nation, is still a part of the British Commonwealth of Nations. Why did the Canadian colonies remain loyal to England while the 13 colonies to the south revolted? You now know the main reasons for the American Revolution. To find out why there was no corresponding revolution in the Canadian colonies, you will have to do some research in your school or community library. Consult the card catalog for books on Canadian history, focusing on the latter half of the 18th century. Then report to the class on your findings.

6. Some students might research actual examples of tyranny (defining it as "a denial of human rights") and report on how people reacted to it. Possible examples include: Stalinism, American slavery, Idi Amin's Uganda, Greek military rule, white rule in South Africa.

7. Governments provide many different services. Our federal government, for example, has many publications (some free) that provide useful information for farmers, business people, labor groups, homemakers, young people, and others. You might find some of these publications helpful in learning more about citizenship and government. You can obtain a list of the publications by writing to: Assistant Public Printer, Superintendent of Documents, Government Printing Office, Washington, D.C. 20402. Your class might order some publications from the list to help form a reference shelf on citizenship.

5: THE FOUNDING FATHERS DISAGREE

The individuals on the opposite page are some of our nation's "Founding Fathers." One of them was a military leader; another signed the Declaration of Independence. Under their leadership, the new American nation had survived the crisis of revolution and war with Britain. But could they lead the country through a second crisis — the crisis of keeping the 13 states together as one nation?

To handle this second crisis, 55 men traveled over muddy roads and choppy seas to meet in Philadelphia in the summer of 1787. They were delegates to a convention representing 12 states. The 13th state, Rhode Island, refused to send anyone. It feared that the other delegates might want to change the American system of government from top to bottom. And that's exactly what many delegates meant to do.

The picture here shows five delegates gathered outside the Philadelphia State House. Who were these men?

Delegate A. A serious young scholar from Virginia. Blue eyes, ruddy cheeks, hair almost gone, even though he was only 33 years old. Later known as the "Father of the Constitution" because he did more than any other delegate to create the Constitution and argue for it. Later to be elected the fourth President of the United States.

Delegate B. The most famous and widely respected delegate. A tall man who seldom smiled. Plantation owner in Virginia. Formerly commander of American forces in the Revolutionary War. Later to be elected the first President of the United States.

Delegate C. Young genius from New York. Thin body, handsome face, clever mind. Worked closely with Delegate B during the Revolution. Later to be first Secretary of the *Treasury**— and after that, to be killed by a bullet from Aaron Burr's dueling pistol.

Delegate D. The shortest delegate (five foot, two inches). Irish-born. One of the ablest graduates of Princeton College. Much admired by the other delegates for his speaking ability. A city in New Jersey is named after him.

Delegate E. The oldest delegate (81 years old). World-famous for his experiments with electricity. Started career as a printer and writer of the humorous *Poor Richard's Almanac*. Sick with gout, he had to be carried to the convention in a sedan chair.

How many of these delegates can you identify? (Your teacher can tell you their names.)

The big question: one nation or 13 separate states? Fifty-five delegates came to Philadelphia with different answers to one big question. Was the United States to be:

a. one nation with one government?

b. 13 states with 13 governments?

c. both one nation and 13 states?

Almost nobody except Alexander Hamilton thought **a** was the best answer. Most Americans probably wanted **c**, but if they couldn't get it, they would rather have **b** than **a**.

Almost all Americans in 1787 felt greater loyalty to their state governments than to the national government. In colonial days, it had been the local and state governments that raised taxes, voted laws, ran the courts, and issued money. Most people continued to think of their state government as the only one that really mattered.

After all, no U.S. national government had existed before 1776. Then, for 10 years after independence, a Congress had met to discuss laws and policies for all the states.

During most of this time, the new nation had tried to function under a written plan called the "Articles of Confederation." Under this plan,

Congress was feeble and helpless. It could only *ask* the states to cooperate. It could not command obedience or cooperation. State legislatures rarely gave the Congress all the tax money Congress asked for. Often the legislatures gave a fraction of what was asked for — or nothing at all. Each state had the power to ignore Congress if it wished to do so.

For several years, a weak Congress was all that the citizens of the different states would accept. But the

JOIN, or

N. E.

D I E.

states began to quarrel with each other, and this led to many problems.

Rhode Island printed paper money that was worth little enough in Rhode Island — and worth almost nothing the minute you crossed the border into Massachusetts. A New Jersey farmer couldn't sell his hogs in New York without paying New York an *import duty** at the state border. In western Massachusetts, a group of farmers took up arms against Massachusetts tax officials. Congress was powerless to do anything about it. Several states tried to create their own navies, even though they lacked money to pay the shipbuilders. It was easy to imagine a day when the navy of South Carolina might fire a few cannonballs at the navy of New York. As things got worse, it was becoming foolish to even talk of a "United" States of America.

The cartoon here pictures the feelings that many of the delegates must have had. It was one of the first cartoons created in the American colonies. Benjamin Franklin drew it in 1754 to try to get the colonies to unite against the French and Indians. Then, during the Revolutionary War, Paul Revere made an engraving of it to help persuade the colonies to unite against England. At that time, many people believed that a snake cut in pieces could live if its parts were put back together.

You might try drawing a cartoon of your own, picturing the situation of the "United" States when the Constitutional Convention met in 1787.

How to be fair to all of the states.

Could the Founding Fathers, meeting in Philadelphia, make a nation out of 13 quarreling states? It was quite a problem.

All 55 delegates believed that Congress was too weak to hold the country together. They agreed that Congress should be given more power. At the same time, all except Hamilton thought the state governments should be strong and independent. But to make Congress stronger, they had to weaken the states. And if they weakened the states, wouldn't they also destroy the states' independence?

A second problem was just as hard to solve: how to create a Congress in which people in the bigger states and people in the smaller states would *both* be fairly represented. To understand how difficult this problem was, think of four different people who lived in 1787.

First, think of Abigail Thomas, a 55-year-old shopkeeper from Delaware. Abigail comes from the smallest of the 13 states. The total population of the state is about 60,000; this includes 9,000 slaves.

Then, think of Karl Muller, a 26-year-old farmer from western Pennsylvania. His state is one of the largest. It has about 430,000 people, including almost 4,000 slaves.

Third, think of George Washington, a 55-year-old Virginia plantation owner. Virginia is by far the largest state with almost 700,000 people,

THREE DIFFERENT PLANS

	Delaware	Pennsylvania	Virginia
Plan A. All states are represented equally in Congress.	Delaware citizens elect one representative.	Pennsylvania citizens elect one representative.	Virginia citizens elect one representative.
Plan B. States send representatives to Congress according to total population.	Delaware citizens elect one representative.	Pennsylvania citizens elect seven representatives.	Virginia citizens elect 12 representatives.
Plan C. States send representatives to Congress according to number of *free* citizens.	Delaware citizens elect one representative.	Pennsylvania citizens elect seven representatives.	Virginia citizens elect seven representatives.

including nearly 300,000 slaves.

Fourth, think of Sally, a 30-year-old woman who works as a slave in George Washington's plantation house. Because she is a slave, she has no last name.

Suppose that each of these four people wants as much influence as possible on the making of the nation's laws. Each wants to make sure that he or she is represented fairly in the new United States government. But what's fair to Abigail Thomas may seem very unfair to Karl Muller. What seems fair to George Washington may not seem fair to Sally.

For example, Virginia has about 12 times as many people as Delaware. Should Virginia therefore also have 12 times as much power as Delaware? Should it have 12 times as many representatives in Congress? Would such a plan be fair to the citizens of Delaware?

The citizens of Delaware might point out that Virginia has almost half as many slaves as free citizens. Maybe a state's power in Congress should depend only on its *free* population. If so, Virginia's power in the national government would drop sharply — and Delaware's power would rise.

The table above shows three plans for representing the people of Virginia, Delaware, and Pennsylvania in Congress. One plan would make Abigail Thomas happy, by giving Delaware citizens more power than the other two plans give them. A second plan would probably be best for Karl Muller and other citizens of Pennsylvania. And George Washington of Virginia would be served best by a third plan. Can you tell which plan is best for which person?

Would any of these plans be fair to a person like Sally? Can you think of any plan that would be equally fair to everyone? The job of the Founding Fathers was to try to create such a plan.

Virginia delegates propose a plan. It was raining on the 29th of May 1787. Early that morning, George Washington led a group of delegates into a room in Independence Hall in Philadelphia. The curtains in the room were drawn, and the doors were locked and guarded.

On this first day of their convention, the delegates agreed that the public should know nothing about their meeting and plans until their work was finished. They also agreed that George Washington should preside over the daily meetings.

But after this first day, the delegates stopped agreeing with each other — and started arguing. Throughout the summer, they argued about a plan suggested by the delegates of Virginia. This plan gave a lot of power to a new national government and not much to the states. And it gave more power to the big states than to the small states. It was, in fact, very much like Plan B. Pennsylvania delegates were satisfied with the plan even though it counted slaves as part of the population.

90

Independence Hall

The short play below might be acted out in class. It is based on real events that took place in the first three weeks of the 1787 Philadelphia Convention. Several of the lines are imaginary. After acting out the play, try to figure out which parts of it are factual and which parts probably did not happen. (Your teacher can tell you the answer.)

THE SUMMER OF '87

James Wilson: a delegate from Pennsylvania

Benjamin Franklin: a delegate from Pennsylvania

George Washington: a delegate from Virginia

William Paterson: a delegate from New Jersey

Luther Martin: a delegate from Maryland

Alexander Hamilton: a delegate from New York

Scene: A room inside the Philadelphia State House. The room is hot and humid, but the windows are closed to prevent curious citizens or newspapermen from hearing the *debates.** Washington sits in a tall chair at the front of the room. Franklin and Wilson are seated together at the same table. The others are seated at the tables of their separate state *delegations.**

Time: Late afternoon on a day in June 1787.

Wilson (*speaking to Franklin in a loud whisper*): Psst, Ben, Ben. The heat in here is killing me. You're an inventor. Can't you think of a gadget of some sort that will cool this room?

Franklin (*whispering*): Of course, why not? Lend me a piece of paper. I'll work on it.

Washington: May I ask for silence from the Pennsylvania delegates? The honorable delegate from New Jersey has the floor.

Paterson: I thank the most honorable chairman. For the past few days, we have been debating a plan from the Virginia delegation. We all know that this plan can never pass. New Jersey and the other smaller states are united against it.

I therefore beg the delegates to consider a second plan. First, I propose a Congress with one chamber, not two. Second, all states shall be equally represented in that chamber. Third, the representatives shall be chosen by the legislatures of the states, not by the people. Fourth, the

Wilson: Psst, Ben. The heat in here is killing me.

executive shall be allowed only one term of office. Fifth, the state governors may, at any time, vote to remove the national executive from office. I believe my plan is more practical than the Virginia plan. It will strengthen the national government without threatening the separate existence of the states.

Washington: The chair recognizes the honorable delegate from Maryland.

Martin: I thank the most honorable chairman. And I thank Mr. Paterson for his sensible and practical plan. A sound plan of government. Very sound. There is no hope for the Virginia plan. None at all. None whatsoever. Do I repeat myself? Well then, so be it. I will tell you now and I will tell you again — I cannot ac-

cept any part of the Virginia plan. I tell you that if you pass any part of it, I shall walk out of this convention. Walk right out that door there. To conclude, I propose that we take up this New Jersey plan without any more delay.

Washington: The chair recognizes the honorable delegate from Pennsylvania.

Wilson: I cannot believe that Mr. Paterson and Mr. Martin are serious. Why, their plan makes a mockery of our purpose here. What's the difference between the one-house Congress in this new plan and the one-house Congress — or rather, the one-house joke — that we've now got? The national government would be just as weak as ever. The small

states could thumb their noses at it, just as they're doing now.

I can understand why a state like New Jersey would want such a plan. But why would the great state of Pennsylvania want it? No, this New Jersey plan is not sensible. It is not sensible, not sound, and not right.

Franklin (*whispering loudly*): Nice speech, my friend.

Wilson: Thank you. But look how it's made me sweat. Have you invented a new cooling system yet?

Franklin: Not yet. But I've got one interesting idea.

Washington: I beg the Pennsylvania delegates to keep silent. The chair recognizes the honorable delegate from New York.

Hamilton: Until now, I have not stood up to speak. I had thought that other delegates, older and wiser than myself, should be allowed to speak first. But I can be silent no longer.

In my opinion, the Virginia plan is weak; and the New Jersey plan is weaker. This nation needs a strong and unified government. We cannot be united if we are divided into 13 states. Therefore, I suggest that we have no state governments at all.

Wilson (*whispering to Franklin*): He's crazy. The heat must have gotten to him.

Hamilton: Instead, we should have only one government. A national government much like the one in Britain. Elect someone to be President for life. Elect members of a Senate to serve life terms. Elect members of an Assembly to serve for three-year terms. Some people may say this is too much like the British monarchy. But we must take that risk. A government that is too strong is better than a government that is too weak.

Washington: The chair recognizes the honorable delegate from Maryland.

Martin: Do you mean, then, to destroy the states? The 13 independent states of America. I cannot stand for it. I think I should walk out of this convention right now.

Wilson (*half whispering*): And good riddance to you.

Martin: What was that, sir? Did I hear myself insulted? I will not stand for it.

Washington: You are out of order, Mr. Martin. I see that it is time to *adjourn.** Mr. Franklin, you have one last word to add? Please make it brief.

Franklin: A fellow delegate has asked me to think of an idea for cooling this room. I know of no gadget or mechanical device that can do it. But I think the best way to cool this room is to cool the tempers of the delegates. Therefore, I suggest that we hire a *chaplain** to lead us in prayer every morning before our debates.

Washington: Does anyone wish to comment on Mr. Franklin's idea? Mr. Hamilton, you may have the last word before we adjourn.

Hamilton: May I remind Mr.

Franklin of one practical difficulty. We have no money to pay a chaplain! I suggest we would do just as well to pray in private.

Washington: This convention stands adjourned until 10 o'clock tomorrow morning. Mr. Martin, I believe you offered to lead us through that door. As we leave, let us pray that both this room and our tempers will be cooler tomorrow morning.

Wilson: Amen.

As this scene ends, it looks as if the convention may break apart. Delegates are not listening to each other. Instead, they are shouting and threatening. How will they ever succeed in writing a constitution that all can accept?

Here are four possible ways to stop the convention from falling apart. In *your* opinion, which action would be most helpful? Which would be least helpful?

1. Alexander Hamilton should apologize for the speech he made.

2. George Washington should tell Luther Martin to leave the convention.

3. William Paterson of New Jersey should bargain with James Madison of Virginia. Paterson can offer to give up some of his plan if Madison gives up some of the Virginia plan.

4. The convention should open with a prayer every morning, as Franklin suggested.

Perhaps you have a better suggestion. If so, discuss it with the class.

"THE LAST WORD"

by Forrest McDonald

The Founding Fathers were unusually intelligent and able men. In addition to their talents, something else may have set them apart from most of their fellow Americans. A historian named Forrest McDonald studied the economic background of each delegate to the Philadelphia convention. In the passages below, adapted from his book We, the People, *he describes the five delegates pictured on page 82.*

Alexander Hamilton. As the son-in-law of the wealthy Philip Schuyler, Hamilton could easily have made a fortune. Instead, he devoted himself to public life, almost totally neglecting his family and private income. He was always in debt.

William Paterson. Son of an Irish *immigrant** who brought him to America in 1747, when he was two years old. His father was a peddler and owner of a store in Princeton, New Jersey. The young Paterson trained in the law at Princeton. But in 1770 his income from four cases of law was only 15 shillings, four pence. After two years, he went into a store with his brother, practicing law only part time.

Benjamin Franklin. Printer, scientist, inventor, statesman, philosopher. At the time of the Convention, he was 81. During his long and eventful life he had built up an estate worth $150,000 — mostly in land and houses.

George Washington. He is usually assumed to have been the richest man in America. . . . There is no doubt that he had a tremendous fortune in land and slaves. However, he had little cash, often borrowed from friends, and was rarely out of debt.

James Madison. He knew more about the theory of money than how to acquire it. He depended on public salaries, gifts from his father, and loans or gifts from friends. His own estate consisted mainly of 560 ill-kept acres in Orange County, Virginia. It was valued at $725. He had six adult slaves, three slave children, and five horses.

(YOU HAVE THE LAST WORD)

What can you say about these five delegates to the Philadelphia Convention? Which statement seems to you to be most accurate?

1. Most were unusually wealthy and free from financial worries.

2. Most were unusually wealthy — but also had serious money problems.

3. The delegates came from mixed backgrounds. A few were unusually wealthy, but most were not.

4. They were concerned with more *important* things than money.

Is it important how much wealth the Founding Fathers had? Would you respect them any more — or less — if they had been farmers, laborers, and shopkeepers?

"CHECKOUT"

Key terms

Articles of Confederation Congress
import duty executive

Review

1. List four examples of problems arising from a weak national government under the Articles of Confederation.

2. What big question did the delegates to the Constitutional Convention face — and what were three possible answers?

3. Describe the conflict between large and small states at the Constitutional Convention.

4. Describe three plans for electing representatives to Congress.

5. Explain how the Virginia plan would affect states like Delaware and New Jersey.

6. How would Hamilton's plan have affected the power of the states?

Discussion

1. If you had been a delegate to the Constitutional Convention, which plan would you have favored: the Virginia plan, Paterson's plan, Hamilton's plan, or some other plan? Why?

2. Why, in your opinion, were most Americans, after the Revolutionary War, against a strong national government?

3. William Paterson of New Jersey proposed, among other things, that (a) the representatives in Congress should be chosen by the legislatures of the states and (b) the executive should be allowed only one term of office. Do you agree with one — or both — ideas? Why or why not?

4. The conflict between those who emphasize a strong national government and those who emphasize state's rights has continued up to 1980. In recent decades, those who put more emphasis on national power have — with the possible exception of the Eisenhower years (1953–1961) — been in control in Washington. But their control is being widely challenged as the 1980's begin. You might clip newspaper articles in which political leaders attack — or defend — "big government" in Washington. Read the most significant of these to the class. Then a panel might lead a discussion of these questions: *Is the national government too powerful? Is it exercising too much control over our lives? Should some of its activities be turned over to state and local governments? Or do we need less of all kinds of government controls?*

Activities

1. Some of you might write a short, imaginative essay or story based on the idea: *What would have happened if we had become 13 separate countries?* (If you do not live in one of the 13 original states, imagine what country your state would belong to — and go on from there.)

2. You might volunteer to research the views of various Founding Fathers on slavery. You might focus on this question: *Why were some of those opposed to slavery willing to agree to the three-fifths compromise?* You should report your findings to the class.

3. You might draw up a plan for celebrating the Constitution's bicentennial in 1987. What would be the major national festivities? How could your local community participate?

4. If there are artists in your class, they might look up a picture of one of the Founding Fathers and do a caricature like the ones in this chapter. The drawings could then be posted on the bulletin board.

5. If you are from one of the original 13 states (other than Rhode Island), you might research the delegates who represented your state at the Constitutional Convention and report your findings to the class. Students from other states might choose one of the delegates mentioned in the text, find out as much as they can about his life and his role at the Convention, and write an essay or outline a talk about him.

6. You might be interested in learning more about the Articles of Confederation under which our new nation was governed from 1781 to 1789. Using good encyclopedias, you could research the topic, focusing on the strengths and weaknesses of the Articles, achievements during the period, and events such as Shay's Rebellion which helped to convince leaders of the new nation that a stronger federal government was needed.

7. You might volunteer to read one of the books (listed on page 117) about the Constitution and the people who helped to create it. Afterward, you could discuss some of your findings with the class.

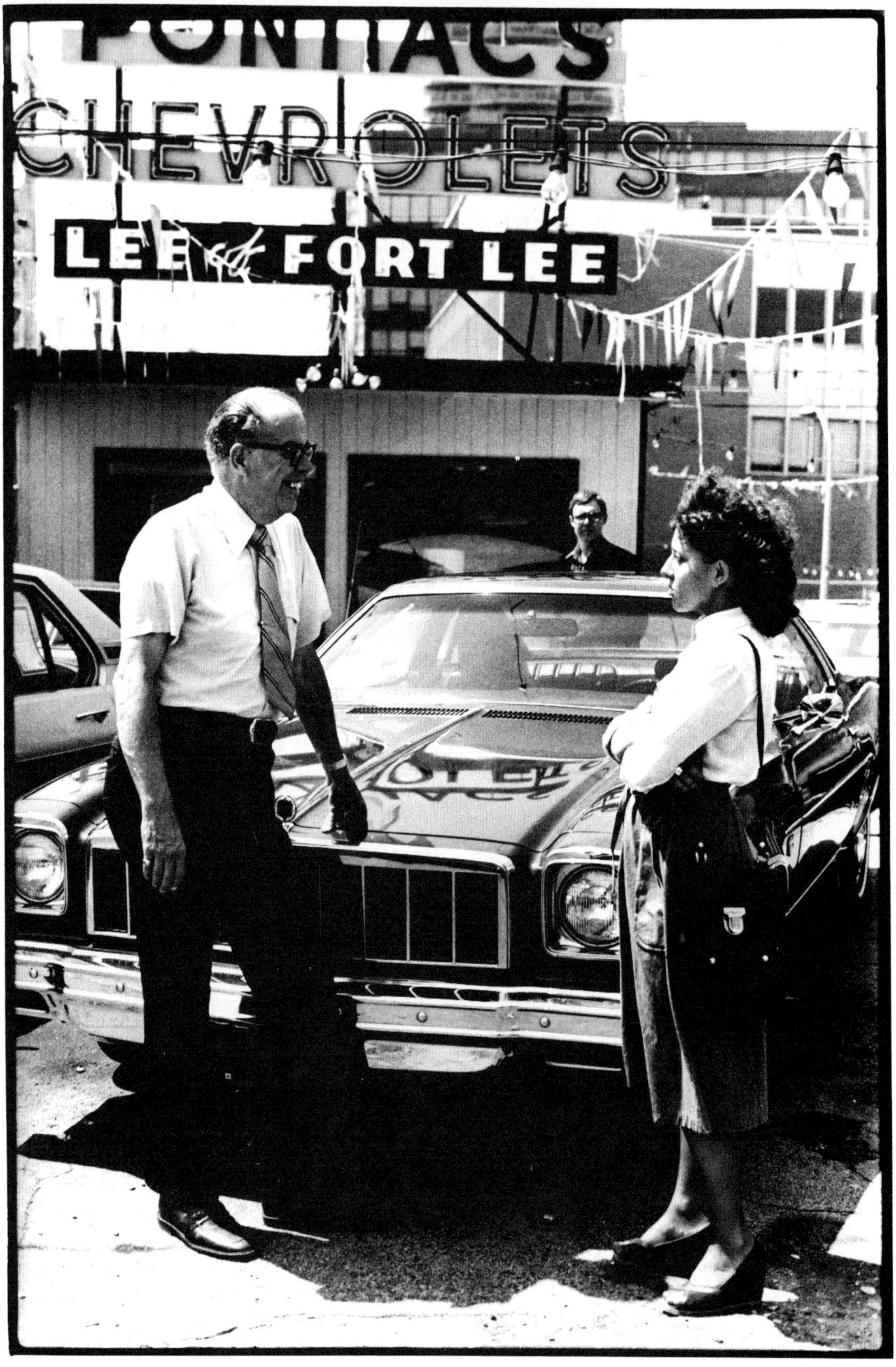
CHEVROLETS
LEE FORT LEE

6: COMPROMISE AND THE CONSTITUTION

A salesperson in a used-car lot will tell you that there are two types of customers. The first type demands a "perfect car" and will settle for nothing less. The second type wants a "good solid car" but is prepared to overlook certain defects if the price is right. You might call the first type a "perfectionist" and the second type a *"compromiser.*"

A dialogue between the salesperson and Ms. Perfectionist might go something like this:

Ms. Perfectionist: The car I'm looking for can be no older than a 1977 model. It can't have more than 40,000 miles on it. I want it to have power brakes, power steering, and standard transmission. It should have whitewall tires and air conditioning. I won't spend more than $2,800 for it. The paint job should look brand new. What have you got to show me?

Salesperson: I've got just the car for you. Look at this Chevelle, 1977 model. Mint condition. Not a scratch on it. Step inside. See how it feels. You're not going to find a

101

COMPROMISER 1 2 3 4 5

sweeter car for the money any-
where.

Ms. Perfectionist: I told you I
wanted standard transmission,
whitewalls, and air conditioning.
And what's this? The price marked
here is $3,200.

Salesperson: It's yours for $2,999.

Ms. Perfectionist: I will not haggle
over the price or anything else. Is
this all you've got to show me?
Then I'll go elsewhere. Thank you.
   (*Ms. Perfectionist walks off.
Another customer, Mr. Compromiser, has been waiting for the
salesperson's attention.*)

Mr. Compromiser: Pardon me.

Salesperson: Yes, sir. What can I do
for you?

Mr. Compromiser: I'm looking for a
medium-priced car, around $2,700,
that's got pretty low mileage. Not too
old, but well-built — solid. Not too
many bumps or scratches. I was

thinking maybe I'd like a Volkswa-
gen.

Salesperson: Well, we just sold our
last VW. But we do have a Chevy I
know you'd like. Only a few
thousand miles on it. Honey of a car.
Absolutely solid. Would you like
to see it?

Mr. Compromiser: Sure, why not.
But you'll have to make me a good
deal.

Salesperson: Here it is. Take a look.
Not a scratch on it. Under the
hood, it's tight as a drum. And it's
very fairly priced at $3,200.

Mr. Compromiser: Looks good.
But I wanted a VW. And the price
on this is a little high for me.

Salesperson: You can't go wrong with
this Chevy. Tell you what I'll do.
If you buy it today, I'm pretty sure
we can strip $200 off the price
without too much trouble. I guarantee you won't find a better car

PERFECTIONIST
6   7   8   9   10

for the money. What did you say
your name was, sir?

Mr. Compromiser: Compromiser.
Charlie Compromiser.

Salesperson: Step right this way, Mr.
Compromiser. We'll see what our
financial manager can do for you.

Mr. Compromiser: Fair enough.
That's a pretty good-looking Chevy,
all right.

Are you the kind of person who
holds out for exactly what you want
or the kind who accepts less if it
seems the best you *might* get? In
short, are you a perfectionist or a
compromiser?

Think of real situations where you
have behaved as a perfectionist
would — or as a compromiser would.
Then, using the chart above, choose a
number between **1** and **10** that best
describes your usual behavior. (The
higher the number, the closer you

are to being a perfectionist.)

Now, you might want to discuss
this question with the class: Is it
better to be a perfectionist or a
compromiser?

As you'll see in this chapter, both
perfectionists and compromisers are
necessary in a democratic government. Both were necessary in the
making of the U.S. Constitution.

**Compromisers and
perfectionists, 1787.** What would
have happened in 1787 if all the
Founding Fathers had been perfectionists? There would probably have
been no Constitution. The tempers in
the Philadelphia State House might
never have cooled off. As perfectionists, the delegates would have
lost patience with each other as soon
as they learned that their opinions
were so different.

For example, the Virginia delegates

demanded a two-house Congress. The New Jersey delegates demanded a one-house Congress. There would have been no way to get these delegates to agree to a common plan. Probably everyone would have walked out of the convention in less than a week.

Fortunately, there were enough perfectionists among the delegates in Philadelphia to force everyone to think hard about every problem. But there were also enough compromisers in the room to suggest a middle ground between seemingly opposite ideas and plans. The best example of how this latter group worked was the so-called *great compromise** between the small states and the big states.

Virginia's delegates had proposed two houses of Congress, each house to have more representatives from the states with more people. Then William Paterson of New Jersey had spoken up for the states with fewer people. He said there should be only one house of Congress. And each state, no matter how many people it had, should be equally represented.

For many weeks, the delegates argued about these two plans. They could not agree as to which plan was better.

The great compromise. How can a conflict like this be settled? Only people with a talent for compromise can suggest a way out.

Roger Sherman, a delegate from Connecticut, had this talent. He knew that delegates from the large states would have to give up part of their favorite plan. And the delegates from the smaller states would have to give up part of their plan. This was Sherman's idea for a compromise plan:

Part 1. Divide Congress into two houses. Call one house the Senate and the other the House of Representatives.

Part 2. Let all states be represented equally in the Senate. Give even the smallest state of Delaware two Senators. And allow each of the other states the same number — two.

Part 3. Let power in the House of Representatives depend upon a state's population. In this house, give Delaware only one representative and give Virginia 10 representatives. Give to the other states a number between one and 10, according to their population. Then, once every 10 years, count the population of each state. Change the number of representatives allowed each state as the state's population grows either bigger or smaller.

Two parts of Roger Sherman's compromise come from the Virginia plan. One part comes from the New Jersey plan. Can you tell which is which? If you were a citizen of Delaware, would you be satisfied with Sherman's compromise plan?

The three-fifths compromise. But Sherman's plan was incomplete. It said nothing about how slaves should be counted. The Southern states would end up with more power in the House of Representatives if slaves could be counted in a state's total population.

Delegates at Philadelphia finally decided on another compromise. (To most of us today, this compromise no doubt seems a tragic — and cruel — mistake. Among other things, it should remind us that not all compromises are good, and many involve a "solution" that may be less than the ideal one.) The delegates decided that only part of the slave population should be counted. A state could include three fifths of its slaves in its total population.

To understand how this worked, figure out the following problem. Suppose classes in your school are represented in a student Congress according to class size.

Class A has 25 "free" students and 15 "slave" students.

Class B has 36 "free" students and no "slave" students.

If only three fifths of the "slaves" can be counted, what is the population of Class A? Which class can send more representatives to the student Congress? Why? (Your teacher can give you the answers.) Suppose you — as a delegate in Philadelphia in 1787 — disliked the three-fifths plan. Suppose you — like George Mason of Virginia — wanted a plan of government that would make slavery illegal. Would you then reject the whole Constitution because it allowed slavery to exist? Would you accept it because you liked most of the Constitution? Would you do something else? Explain what position you would take — and why.

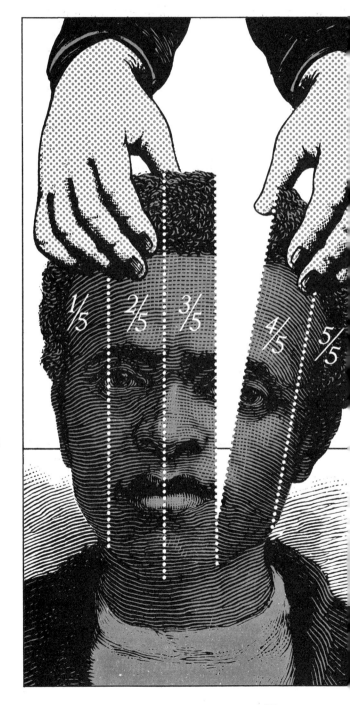

Signing the Constitution. For three hot summer months, the delegates at Philadelphia debated their plans and compromises. They argued fiercely for their own ideas. Several, including Luther Martin, angrily walked out of the convention.

But finally the delegates produced a complete new plan of government. They called it the "Constitution of the United States." It included both Sherman's compromise and the three-fifths compromise. Hand-lettered by a master penman, the document was now ready for the delegates' signatures.

Yet even now, on the last day of the convention, many delegates found it hard to accept different parts of the Constitution. The oldest delegate, Ben Franklin, tried to coax these unhappy delegates into signing. He said that he too saw faults in the Constitution. But he thought he could learn to live with them. And perhaps, after a while, he might change his mind and even approve of the things which he now saw as faults.

At least three delegates in the room bitterly disagreed. Edmund Randolph of Virginia, George Mason of Virginia, and Elbridge Gerry of Massachusetts saw too many faults in the Constitution. They refused to sign their names to it. But they were outnumbered by 39 delegates who believed the Constitution would at least work better than the weak one-house Congress. On September 17, 1787, they solemnly signed their names to the document they had created and left Philadelphia for home.

Fighting for your rights, 1788.
A new plan of government had been created at Philadelphia. But was it any good? Was it really any better than the old, weak one-house Congress? Many people, when they first read the Constitution in their newspapers, thought it was terrible. How could George Washington sign such a thing? they wondered.

Where, they asked, was there any statement in this Constitution about people's rights? All the constitutions of the different states included a list of rights — a *bill of rights.** But there was no bill of rights in the U.S. Constitution. No guarantee of a fair trial in a U.S. court. No guarantee of religious freedom. No guarantee that a citizen could speak freely without being thrown in jail. No guarantee that a newspaper would be allowed to print editorials that criticized the government.

The people had fought for their rights in the Revolution of 1776. Now they wondered if they would lose everything through this Constitution that seemed to ignore their rights.

At the time, some Americans were not worried. They were willing to accept the Constitution, with or without a bill of rights. But which group was stronger — the perfectionists who demanded a bill of rights, or the compromisers who could accept the Constitution without change?

Citizens both for and against the Constitution prepared for a great struggle. Each was determined to win. No contest in American history was more important than this one.

The rules of the contest were simple enough. Nine of the 13 states had to approve or *ratify** the Constitution if it was to be the new law of the land. In each state, there would be a special convention of delegates to debate the Constitution and vote "yes" or "no" on ratification.

Imagine that your class is one of these ratifying conventions. How many members of the class would vote for the Constitution even though it lacked a bill of rights? How many would vote against it?

First, read the two advertisements on the following pages. Then, after discussion, take a class vote on the question: Should the Constitution be ratified?

Now let's see what actually happened to the proposed new Constitution when its fate was being decided by the 13 state conventions.

Delaware acted first. All 30 of the delegates to its convention voted in favor of ratification. Pennsylvania followed, after a bitter quarrel between delegates. New Jersey, Georgia, Connecticut were for ratifying, even without a bill of rights.

Then came Massachusetts' turn. Here, in the state where the Revolution had begun, most of the delegates were ready to vote no. They demanded a bill of rights and would settle for nothing less. If Massachusetts voted no, Virginia and New York would probably vote no too.

The time had come for one last compromise. "Go ahead and draw up a bill of rights," said the Massachusetts supporters of the Constitution. "We guarantee that this will be the first piece of business of the new Congress."

The offer worked. It changed the minds of enough delegates to cause Massachusetts to vote for ratification by the close vote of 186–168. Other states followed Massachusetts' example; they would vote for ratification *if and only if* a bill of rights was to be added later.

Eventually, all 13 states ratified the Constitution. The United States in 1788 had a new government, consisting of a President, a two-house Congress, and a *Supreme Court.**

Finally, in 1791, 10 *amendments** that guaranteed all Americans freedom from unfair treatment by government officials were added to the Constitution. These first 10 amendments were more generally known as the Bill of Rights. The first Congress under the Constitution had lived up to the promises made for it.

The United States of America now had the most democratic plan of government in the world. Of course there were still weaknesses in the plan. But these too were later corrected. Today many people think the Constitution is a masterpiece.

They think it is one of the most useful inventions ever created by the human mind — even more useful than the telephone or the automobile. Why do you think they respect it so much?

Vote NO!

Vote YES!

ANNOUNCING AN ALL-NEW PLAN OF GOVERNMENT!

The Constitution of the United States.

Featuring:

• A strong and independent President . . . someone to lead us.

• A more powerful two-house Congress . . . able to make the laws that you need so badly.

• A Supreme Court . . . able to guarantee justice for all.

What makes this plan of government better than the old one?

Everything!

At last, you'll have money in your pocket that's worth something in every state.

At last, you'll have a strong government that can defend you from foreign enemies.

At last, there will be a real President — someone to enforce the laws of Congress.

Why should you trust the Constitution?

Because it was created by people you can trust. Who can doubt the ability of George Washington of Virginia? Who can doubt the wisdom of Benjamin Franklin of Pennsylvania? Who can doubt the genius of Alexander Hamilton of New York?

They created the Constitution.

They signed it.

Now all you have to do is vote for it.

Vote YES on ratification!

Do you value your freedom?

The Constitution could take it away. Don't let it happen.

They say that the new government will have more power. But just think. Do you want a more powerful government? You have little enough control over your state government. Think how much less control you will have over laws made by a distant national government.

They say that the old government doesn't work. Of course our government has weaknesses. We all know that. But can't we repair it?

They say you should trust this new government to respect your rights. Why should you trust it? This Constitution says nothing about your rights. To protect you against harm, all state constitutions list your rights. Why has this national Constitution failed to list them?

What can you gain from this new government? Very little.

What can you lose? A great deal — including your freedom.

Vote NO on ratification

You've seen how the U.S. Constitution was written and adopted. You now have the knowledge to write a constitution of your own. Use the constitution here as your starting point. It suggests one plan for governing your school. Like the U.S. Constitution, this plan describes the power that different people shall have over the government. It also states how the constitution shall be ratified or adopted.

As you study the proposed constitution, ask yourself these questions:

1. Which parts, if any, do you like?

2. Which parts, if any, do you object to?

3. What changes would you make?

4. Should a bill of rights be added to the constitution? Would these rights be for students only — or for teachers and other school personnel as well?

5. Do you think a constitution like this would ever be ratified by the four different groups — parents, teachers, students, and the School Board?

Discuss these questions with other students.

On the chalkboard, write all the changes or additions members of your class propose to the constitution. Then take a vote on these proposed changes. Finally, find out whether two thirds of the students in your class would approve the constitution as changed.

We, the people of _____ school, in order to form a more perfect government, do ordain and establish this constitution.

ARTICLE I. POWER OF THE STUDENTS.

Section 1. During the first week of school, every homeroom class shall elect three student officers. These officers shall have the power to speak and act for the needs of all students enrolled in the school. They shall be called the Class Senate.

Section 2. The Class Senate shall meet together every Friday during one regular class period.

Section 3. The Class Senate shall have power to recommend to the principal all rules concerning student dress and conduct in the school. The principal may approve or veto any recommended rule. But the Class Senate may, by a two-thirds vote of all members, override his or her veto.

ARTICLE II. POWER OF THE TEACHER.

Section 1. The teacher shall have complete power to decide whether a student passes or fails a course. But every student shall have the right to appeal a failing grade to a special board consisting of two Senators, two teachers, and the principal.

Section 2. At the end of every month, the teacher shall inform students of their grade average in the course. At the end of every two months, teachers shall inform parents or guardians about each student's work.

ARTICLE III. POWER OF PARENTS AND GUARDIANS.

Section 1. Parents shall have power to examine a teacher's record book at any time. Parents may also visit a class at any time.

Section 2. There must be a hearing attended by a parent or guardian before any student can be suspended or expelled.

ARTICLE IV. RATIFYING THE CONSTITUTION.

Section 1. Four groups must approve this constitution before it becomes law. A convention of teachers must approve it by a two-thirds vote. A convention of students must approve it by a two-thirds vote. A convention of parents must approve it by a two-thirds vote. And the School Board must approve it by a two-thirds vote.

Section 2. The principal shall decide when and how these conventions shall meet.

Robespierre

"THE LAST WORD"

by Robert R. Palmer

Imagine for a minute that events in our nation's history had turned out differently. Instead of writing the Constitution in 1787, suppose the Founding Fathers had written it in 1793. Instead of writing it in Philadelphia, suppose they had written it in Paris, France. Instead of Washington, Franklin, and Madison, suppose the last names of three of our leaders were Robespierre, Saint-Juste, and Couthon. Suppose finally that, instead of a hangman's noose, the government used a machine called a guillotine* to put prisoners to death.

Here is the true story of what happened to some of those who created a new plan of government for France in 1793. The story is adapted from Robert Palmer's book, Twelve Who Ruled.

As you read, ask yourself why the writers of the U.S. Constitution did not suffer a similar fate.

Guardsmen broke suddenly into the room [where Robespierre and his supporters were hiding]. Robespierre's brother climbed out a window, but fell to the street almost dead. The helpless Couthon [lame and unable to walk] plunged down a staircase and injured himself in the head. Saint-Juste yielded without resistance. Le Bas killed himself with a pistol, handing another to Robespierre, who shot himself in the jaw. Some say that Robespierre did not attempt suicide, but was wounded by a soldier.

Saint-Juste and Couthon were held